HELPING YOURSELF WITH ASTROMANCY

Other books by the authors:

The Magic Power of Witchcraft
Meta-Psychometry
Witch's Grimoire of Ancient Omens, Portents, Talismans, Amulets, and Charms
Power Secrets from a Sorcerer's Private Magnum Arcanum

HELPING YOURSELF WITH ASTROMANCY

Gavin Frost and Yvonne Frost

PARKER PUBLISHING COMPANY, INC.
WEST NYACK, N.Y.

PARKER PUBLISHING COMPANY, INC.
WEST NYACK, N.Y.

This book is a reference work based on research by the authors. The opinions expressed herein are not necessarily those of or endorsed by the Publisher.

Library of Congress Cataloging in Publication Data

Frost, Gavin.
Helping yourself with astromancy.

1. Success. 2. Occult sciences. I. Frost, Yvonne, joint author. II. Ibn Saud. III. Title.
BJ1611.2.F72 13180-11780
ISBN 0-13-386243-7

Printed in the United States of America

Dedicated to Sybil Leek, a Witch and one of the world's foremost astrologers.

Astrology represents the summation of all the psychological knowledge of antiquity.

Professor Carl Jung

FOREWORD
by Gavin Frost

In the cool dawn of a tropic day in Lahore, Pakistan, I first heard the words that would result in this book. My Sikh guide and I were playing back the third tape from a recorder we had left running all night in the citadel of the ruins at Mohenjo Daro. Suddenly and clearly, a voice spoke. The astounded guide recognized the language as Hindi, though because of the accent he was unable to translate the words. They were later translated in Karachi. The transcript read:

"I, Ibn Saud, lived in thy plane of existence in the year 480. In my poor time I was considered a great seer and teacher. Some said I was a Holy Man, others, a Sufi; but I did claim neither of these titles, being instead content to help my fellow man. Now I come again, this time in spirit only, to help the poor bewildered people of the world. Verily, it is my hope that my few poor words will help them understand that the ancient astronomic science can and should be used to ease their lives."

Ibn Saud went on to tell of a system of astrology based on astronomy. That system was both simple and exciting, for it held the promise of a technique with which anyone could improve his lot. The information was startling to me because it presented a whole new facet of astrology. That facet was the *use* of astrology to gain whatever you wish from life. As a predictive tool of great power, astrology has been around for centuries; but this sudden new view of the uses to which astrology could be put, and the scathing remarks and scorn with which Ibn Saud treated much modern astrology, were nothing less than shocking.

Almost ten years have now passed in careful testing of Ibn Saud's claims; and in hundreds of cases through the School I have found that what Ibn Saud taught is true and does work.

Did Ibn Saud Live?

The answer to that question is beyond our research capabilities, and beyond the records of the authorities in Lahore (the city closest to Mohenjo Daro.) Of course we could be the victims of a hoax by the Sikh guide who changed the tapes, for he was often alone with the recorder, or by the translator in Karachi. However, for several reasons I think the voice was genuine.

1. The Sikh guide would have had to be a consummate actor to display the terror he did when he first heard the voice of Ibn Saud played back.
2. The translator in Karachi was selected at random; he had little knowledge of astronomy or astrology. In fact he spelled phonetically many words which we eventually recognized as various signs of the zodiac.

It has also been suggested that I may have projected my thoughts onto the tape; but I do not speak Hindi, nor do I have any real knowledge of the language.

Is This a Book Written from beyond the Grave?

In the early 1970's much experimentation was done with a new breakthrough[1] in spirit communication. Occultists everywhere tried the new techniques of tape-recording spirit

---

[1]*Breakthrough*, Dr. Konstantin Raudive, Taplinger Publishing Company, New York.

voices, especially when it was learned that the Christian church (in the person of no less an authority than Pope Paul VI) was interested in the technique and its results, and was tolerant of the work. Many eminent Doctors of Physics and of Theology wrote of their belief in such spirit voices.[2]

THIS BOOK WAS WRITTEN WITH THE AID OF SUCH A VOICE FROM A TAPE.

The whole subject of whether or not spirit voices can really be recorded on tape has been discussed in many books. It is a phenomenon that you can try for yourself. In trying it, we believe you will find, as we did, that there is truth in it.

Unfortunately the actual Mohenjo Daro tapes were left with the translator in Karachi and were destroyed in one of the food riots occurring there in the mid-1970's. Therefore we leave it up to you to decide whether a large part of this book was dictated by a man who died ten centuries ago.

TRY THE EXPERIMENTS HE SUGGESTS. THEY WORK AMAZINGLY WELL.

GAVIN FROST

---

[2]*Voices from the Tapes*, Peter Bander, Drake Publishers Inc., New York.

A NOTE ABOUT THE AUTHORS

Gavin and Yvonne are the leaders of a correspondence School which over the past ten years has taught Witchcraft to many thousands of students. That School, the School of Wicca, is located at P O Box 1502, New Bern, North Carolina 28560. The majority of the examples in this book are drawn from letters written to the School. Because so many thousands of letters arrive every year, Gavin and Yvonne have little chance to verify the authenticity of each individual case history they have cited. The volume of mail convinces them that the systems they teach do work effectively and easily. Those systems work for the Frosts and for their students; Gavin and Yvonne are confident they will work equally well for you.

HOW ASTROMANCY CAN CHANGE YOUR LIFE TO ONE OF CONSTANT REWARD

Don't Blame Yourself

Are you often frustrated because friends don't act the way they promise? Worse yet, are you often thwarted by your own minor mistakes or by the lack of that lucky break that will put you ahead?

IT'S NOT YOUR FAULT

— IT'S NOT THEIR FAULT

Your nature and personality are determined by the time you are born and by your early environment. Everything in this world changes except the nature and personality of man. In his very first remarks Ibn Saud gave us the ancient laws that showed how this is so. In giving that ancient knowledge, he also gave us the method by which your personality can be changed so as to overcome these problems.

The structure of our society is such that a child born at one time of the year is faced with different situations than a child born at another season. Consider the child whose birthday falls just after Christmas. He will always be a little short-changed on toys. He grows up with a permanent chip on his shoulder, always looking at what the other person gets. Richard Nixon is a typical example of this personality. Children born slightly later in the year, when they grow older, become the youngest in their classrooms; consequently they exhibit higher intelligence than average, for they learn early to struggle to keep even. Thus these and other subtle personality differences are inevitable among persons born in successive months of the year. Once you recognize them, you can use these differences to overcome your weaknesses and to gain advantages for yourself.

Science Not Black Art

The great magician Solomon, son of David, decreed that his wise men should be able to tell him

> *the time to sow, the time to reap;*
> *the time to make love, the time to make money;*
> *the time for serene contemplation of the handiwork of the Almighty.*

Solomon knew that the wise men had such information; for, in time so long ago that only the mountains remember it, another king had set Watchers of the Heavens. In this manner did the great towers called 'ziggurats' come to be built in my land. On the topmost spaces of these mighty monuments the Watchers recorded the progress of the great Wheel of the Heavens as it rolled above the ever-changing mountains and deserts; the great Wheel still today rolls above thy very head as thou goest about thy daily tasks.

Hundreds of generations later, when thousands upon thousands of observations had been taken, the wise men saw that not only was there a time suitable for everything, but also that certain of our people, according to the time they were born, were more fitted for certain tasks than for others. Thus the Watchers and the sages of my land did develop a simple system, a system which is beyond the need of writing or of calculation (for most of my people have no stylus or papyrus), a system now called the science of Astronomy.

As generation hath succeeded generation, so this great science hath degenerated into a black art called by many astrology, an art so surrounded by mystic signs and calculations that few can understand or use it aright. Yet, withal, the science is basically simple and still doth work. I am much encouraged that recently astrologers are once again coming into the light and stripping away the superstitions and mystery from the science so that it hath taken on a lighter hue. Much that should be known hath been forever lost. Most vitally important is that part that tells thee how thou canst change thy nature and thy destiny.

Anyone Can Use Astromancy

Astromancy is simplicity itself to use. Before we would believe the voice from beyond the grave, we tested and researched its spectacular claims on hundreds of ordinary people. You will meet more than forty of these people through their case histories as you read of their successes in this book. Let us look at the successes other ordinary people achieved in some of the areas in which you too might want to use Astromancy.

- *Business Success* – In Chapter XII you will learn how Benjie, a ten-year-old, became president of his own company. Surely if a ten-year-old can do it, so can you.
- *Health* – Spencer was so sick he could do almost nothing. Yet, as you will learn in Chapter VI, he is now a company president.
- *Luck and Destiny* – Chapter IV tells how you can be reborn to a new life and how Hal used this technique to gain success.
- *Protection* – Astromancy can provide both psychic and mundane protection for you and for your property. In Chapter IX you will learn how Florella stopped people robbing her and her apartment, and also how Dolores psychically protected herself and drove a Sorcerer berserk.

- *Wealth* – Marvin was an aircraft mechanic. In Chapter XI you will learn how he reaped a $250,000 immediate reward and doubled his money by following an Astromantic plan. You will also meet Friedrich, who used another Astromantic technique to make millions.
- *Friendship, Affection, Love, and Soul-Twinning* – Do you know how to select your friends? Especially long-term friends? Are you, as George was, lonely in a big city? In Chapter VII you will learn how George overcame this problem in a way you too can easily master. Whatever your romantic needs, you can use Astromancy to fulfill them. Once you have found your twin soul, you can bind yourself in perpetual harmony by using the twinning technique.

These are just a handful of the ways that Astromancy can lead you first to magical understanding and then to success in your endeavors.

Change Your Personality for a New Life

Ibn Saud's great new revelation from beyond the grave is that—if you will it—you can change your nature. As you will read in this work, Ibn Saud showed how you can use Astromancy to change both your own and other people's natures, for either a short time or a long one.

Thus instantly and overnight, you can change your personality, your very nature, and hence your life. Hundreds of tests of this claim have been conducted. In every case the person involved gained enormous benefits by making slight changes in his nature. For it is your nature that is your driving force. Whether you wish to be a business leader or a lover, a sports hero or a gourmet cook, merely assume the appropriate nature and you will get the help that will automatically bring to you the success you need and deserve.

The World Changes; Only the Heavens Are Immutable

Once a wise man of my land was invited to a certain city to teach his wisdom to the people dwelling there. When he arrived a great meeting was held in which the city folk proposed to tell him all their problems. The sage held his hand aloft and said, "These are your problems," then proceeded to enumerate the various difficulties of the city and its people. Eventually the Prince of that city threw himself at the feet of the wise man and asked, "By what wondrous magic is it that thou canst tell us all our problems, O great and glorious Prophet?"

The sage directed the Prince to bring a jug of water, some salt, and some flour. Placing the salt and some flour into the water, he asked the Prince, "What is there in this jug that thou canst not see?"

"There is a mixture of salt, flour, and water," the Prince replied.

The Prophet then spake: "Thus it ever was, and thus it ever will be. When people of different ages are brought together and mixed in the closed container of a town, even though each be different their problems will ever be the same; and a stranger, knowing the peoplewho are mixed, will know their problems."

I, Ibn Saud, being a direct descendant of the ancient wise ones, was taught this knowledge seemingly centuries ago. It is this simple form that thou canst use without the need of deadening calculations, which I am now about to expound to thee.

The fathers of thy fathers' fathers, the mothers of thy mothers' mothers, for countless generations reaching back into the ageless time, have been influenced by the great cosmic rhythm, the rhythm which we but dimly perceive as the Wheel of the Heavens moves every day above the timeless sands of the desert. Modern civilizations, built like houses of cards on the oil that comes from below those selfsame sands, have not changed thee. Outwardly thou mayest look different; but in the innermost Thou, thou and all thy friends are just as susceptible to the cosmic rhythms and thus to Astromancy as thou and they ever were. Therefore the knowledge I shall impart to thee will work whether thou livest as I did in a remote village or thou livest in a glass and steel skyscraper in a modern city. The rhythms are changeless. The magic is there for all to see, to experience, and to use. Reach out, my child, not only with a grasping hand but also with a grasping mind; and I will help thee fulfill thyself. Read, understand the ageless, timeless wisdom and power of Astromancy.

Possible Tumor and Arthritis Cures Credited to the Powers

Letters from Student File Y3-8TA

Hundreds and thousands of people write to us as Witches, sending us weird requests and demands. (If you wish to write to us, remember: We do not do such things as money spells or love spells.) These letters and requests we view as rather negative; for with the aid of this book you can do these things easily for yourself. All you have to do is follow the directions. Figure Intro-1 shows two extracts from letters out of the student file we referenced above,[1] letters which show clearly that our techniques work. At the time of going to press, Warren's sister-in-law is still doing well. The fear she felt of cancer is gone completely away.

Another serious and debilitating disease feared by many people is arthritis. We met Dexter M on a trip we made to Durham. When he learned we were open to the idea of the occult, he told us how he had overcome a crippling condition in

---

[1]Most examples in this book are taken from the files of the Church and School of Wicca. In the main they are extracts from student letters. There are so many cases and letters in the files (over 12,000) from people in all walks of life, that we are confident of the correctness of the path we teach and of Ibn Saud's words. We trust the students to tell us the truth in their letters; we hope that you trust them too.

Greetings Yvonne,

Can you advise me? My brother, recently married has a wife with cancer in both lungs & some lymph nodes. She's been given 3 months to live without treatment and 6 months with it.

Blessed be Yvonne,

Warren

Greetings Yvonne,

New news. About two months ago my sister in law was told she had 3 mos to live, with cancer in both lungs, her bones, lymph glands & stomach. I tried healing her, wicca style & wrote you about it. Yesterday she saw the doctor, she is now down to one tumor & it is shrinking. The Dr. says spontaneous remission, but we know. She thanks you, my brother thanks you & I thank you, for opening my eyes & showing me the way.

Blessed be Yvonne,

Warren

Figure Intro-1

his foot. For years he had suffered from arthritis, and following the occult tradition he started to wear copper bracelets on his wrists. Within a week these bracelets began to relieve his discomfort, but then Dexter developed a painful calcium spur on his heel. It became so painful that even though he took some fourteen prescription pain-relieving pills a day, still he could barely walk. He decided he would try to use the Power to heal his foot. Today Dexter needs no pain pills whatsoever.

His physician was puzzled and intrigued by Dexter's experience. From time to time he has asked Dexter to stop his self-cure techniques to see what would happen. Each time he stopped, Dexter's foot regrew the spur and discomfort returned to such an extent that he became unable to walk without the aid of pain pills.

What Can It Hurt?

Even in the life of a millionaire there is room for improvement. Everyone has something that can be helped with our techniques. It may not be as major as saving yourself from the brink of death or from a totally crippling disease; but still when you improve your life so that it becomes more smooth and serene, that serenity will flow from you and make the lives of those around you happier and better. There are many paths to occult knowledge and its awareness. Our path lies through good health, wealth, and happiness. It is no sin to use occult means to get more comfort into your life so that you can study without handicaps the various religious ethics of this world. The Christian Bible,[2] in common with holy books of other religions, is quite clear that these gifts, of healing for instance, are the gifts of God and you should use them with a clear conscience to benefit yourself and the rest of mankind.

If there is evil in the world, that evil is the suppression of knowledge which could help you.

"You have rejected knowledge, and I will reject you."[3] Again, if we turn to the holy books of the world, we see they

---

[2] 1 Corinthians 12.

[3] Hosea 4:6

all agree: You are instructed to study and to gain knowledge throughout your life. The very first chapter of this book will give you knowledge you can put to immediate use. Once you have that knowledge, it will take you but a few minutes to try the procedures we recommend. Even a child can use them. So as soon as you have read Chapter I, why don't you try a few of them in ways that will be of benefit? We predict you can immediately and dramatically improve your life.

Drink Thou of the Cup of Life

The Cup of Life is there for all to drink from, according to their natures. Some drink deeply from only one place on its rim; others sip a little from all round the rim and gain a balanced rhythmic life. My words will help thee gain what thou desirest from the Cup of Life. If thou drinkest deeply from but one place, perhaps the place called 'Wealth,' thou mayest find that thou hast problems because thou hast neglected other places. The rim of the Cup of Life is similar to the Wheel of the Heavens, for in the Wheel of the Heavens there is power to do all that thou desirest.

In my words I will use arcane names for certain almighty power sources in the heavens. The learning of these twelve names will be the most that thou wilt find necessary in availing thyself of all the knowledge enabling thee to drink from any place thou wishest around the rim of the Cup of Life. Verily, thou mayest drink thy fill. Thou mayest live as in the harem of a sheik; or with the wealth of an Ali Baba; thou mayest live with the serenity of a hermit, or be as dynamic as an emir. It is up to thee to choose whether the learning which will lead thee to thy heart's desire is worth the effort. Whatever path thou takest to the mountain top, may the gods guide thy footsteps.

Inshallah!
(As God wills it)

GAVIN FROST AND YVONNE FROST

CONTENTS

Chapter One

RELEASING YOUR ASTROMANTIC POWERS

What This Chapter Will Do for You

- Introduce you to the power of Astromancy
- Tell you why you should never tell anyone your true birthdate
- Show you how to overcome problems easily
- Allow you to try immediately the ancient techniques
- Release your Astromantic powers

Ibn Saud, Our Long-Dead Helper

Many occult and inspirational books like this one have been written with the aid of communication from beyond the grave. This book is unique in that it combines such communication with reports of the practical results modern people have obtained by using the direction received from a long-dead teacher whose name in life was Ibn Saud.

Picture if you will an elderly wizened man in flowing robes of many colors, living almost a thousand years ago. Picture a man keen of eye, erect of bearing, a man who lived a full life and enjoyed it, and who overcame all the problems that the Fates in the form of disease, hardship, robbers, and the deserts could send him. That is the man who we believe communicated with us to guide the writing of this book.

Are you a prisoner of your nature? Are you timid, afraid of change? Unsuccessful in love and romance? Do you never quite make the big score? Ibn Saud's teachings, as explained and expanded in this book, will show you how to change your nature so that you can become instantly successful.

Each unto Himself

In this world of infinite variety there will ever be leaders and followers, workers and scribes. All is in its appointed place. If thou art unsuccessful, mayhap it is because thou dost not follow thy nature, or because thy nature is one which requires thee to follow a profession that gives thee more spiritual reward than riches of the world.

Over countless centuries it hath been noted that people born in different times of the year exhibit different natures. Because of their different inborn natures, people are more successful or less successful at the various tasks they undertake. In recent time it hath become fashionable to advertise thy time of birth by the wearing of amulets and by open discussion of thy characteristics. Canst thou not see how foolish this is? For the leader of men mayhap will think unto himself, "Ah! He is born to be a toiler in the field. He can never succeed in that task for which I seek a leader." The evil Sorcerer too can use that knowledge of thyself—which thou dost freely give—to work against thee.

Yet the shekel hath two faces. For thou canst take unto thyself another nature: one that is fitted for thy success; and by advertising this nature canst gain new positions, wealth, and love, or canst avoid the Evil Eye.

Ned Changes His Nature and Turns Failure into Success

Student File 3Y-2FR

Edward H, known to his friends as Ned, is a public accountant in a small town in Missouri. Ned followed in his father's career footsteps mainly because his father forced him into it. Ned had a light nature and a short interest span, however: qualities ill-suited to such a serious business as accounting. Not that Ned was incompetent; but in his relations with businessmen he tended to wear flashy clothing and spend a lot of time cracking jokes where he should have been soberly discussing profit-and-loss statements and tax advantages. As a consequence, in the normal course of things Ned was only just able to make ends meet. Matters took an abrupt turn for the worse when his office was burned out and it was realized that good old happy-go-lucky Ned had let the insurance premiums lapse. In order to get back on his feet, Ned took out a second mortgage, then a third, on his home. Gradually he had to face the unpleasant fact that his income was never going to pay all the debts he had run up.

We met Ned one night in a local bar just as he was coming to this realization. He felt that what he needed to pull him out of his debt situation was some of Witchcraft's magic; so he signed up for the School's course in basic Witchcraft. In his way, of course, he only lightly brushed over our teaching; thus he did not gain knowledge in sufficient depth to get his life really straightened out. In correspondence with Ned we pointed out emphatically that without serious application he would never succeed in using Witchcraft or any other means to solve his problems. We recommended, therefore, that Ned try to change his nature to a more serious one.

Ned was one of the first people we got to try Ibn Saud's complete method.[1] Though we had some difficulty in getting him pinned down and making him complete the technique, still he finally did it; and for the first time in his life he suddenly began behaving like a businessman and applying all his ability to his life and his work. His wife Beatrice was just amazed. Suddenly she could talk to him seriously; suddenly he began to take note of what she was saying, and would logically discuss alternatives through which they might get out of their financial trouble, rather than avoid discussion by running off in all directions at once.

From that time on, Ned's business prospered. No longer was he the life and soul of the party; instead he was a serious businessman. With his new attitude and his business contacts, he was able to consolidate his loans and pay them off. Today, a few short years later, nearly all the firms in town now depend on Ned's business.

We warned Ned bluntly that the change in his nature would not be permanent and that he should get a capable, serious partner to run the day-to-day operations of the business. Ned hired a college student who was majoring in business administration to be his backup man and to handle the routine work of keeping the books of his clients. These days, Ned is respected as one of the business leaders in his town. He uses his inborn light nature to establish and to maintain customer relations, while his associate handles the clients' accounts on the more serious level.

Change Your Nature and Your Luck Today

All your life long, you may have believed that your lack of success was your own fault. But that is not necessarily true! Until we heard what the wise old sage told us, we too did not realize how easily the nature you are born with can be modified. Admittedly, you can modify that nature only for

---

[1]Fully described in Chapter IV.

short periods; however, these changed periods are quite long enough to woo and marry the mate of your dreams, for instance, or to gain that financial success you have always longed for.

We were not satisfied just to accept what Ibn Saud told us without testing it. Over several years now, we have tried out the technique he recommended with hundreds of people; in well over 90 percent of the cases we have seen dramatic changes in people's natures and successful accomplishment of their life goals. With their previous born-in nature, they could have achieved these successes only with great difficulty—if at all.

Because of the nature that was fixed in you at the time of your birth, you have certain strengths; but for the same reason you have certain weaknesses. The failures you have had in your life are most probably due to those inborn weaknesses. For the first time, with the aid of this book, you will be able to overcome those weaknesses and replace them with strengths. The system we will pass on to you from Ibn Saud is the one that hundreds have used to change their natures and fortunes. You too can get an immediate change in your nature by following our simple directions.

Changing your nature a little bit is a quick and easy process. All you need do is get yourself entirely imbued with the mood of the nature you want to become. Let us say you have been relatively unsuccessful in the romantic encounters you have essayed. In order to guarantee success the next time you want to bring romance into your life, you should behave like a swan gliding over the clear water. If you want to bring in more lust and less romance, you should imagine yourself to have the nature of a scorpion. For most of your needs, simply dressing in the correct mode, wearing the appropriate jewelry, and telling people you have a different birthdate than your true one will accomplish your end. First we will tell you how to make a quick change in your nature; and later we will explain how you can develop your powers so that you can make more enduring changes, both in yourself and in others.

Let out the Animal in Thy Nature

In ancient time, while the Watchers from the ziggurats studied the skies and mankind, it came unto them that the natures of men were like unto the natures of animals. Man had within his heart and body all the natures of all the animals; and yet withal his mind did keep all those animals subservient to his will, just as in the world he doth hold sway both over the beasts he hath tamed and over those which remain wild.

Realization came unto the Watchers that in those persons born at certain times of the year some of the animal natures were more preponderant than others. In order to make the system understandable to the least of our people, the Watchers did use only twelve animals to explain their system.

In the centuries since the Watchers studied the heavens, man's nature hath not changed, even though he now hath many modern marvels. Knowing the animal that thou art like unto, thou canst live in tune with thine own nature, or canst assume the nature of another. If thou dost suppress thine inborn nature for many moons, though, thou shouldst be ware; for that way lies sickness and ill health. Let thy nature out, and thou wilt be serene and happy.

Molly Understands Dr. P and Finds Serenity

Student File G3-OXA

Molly P is a housewife in St. Louis, Missouri; she was previously married to Dr. P—who led her a merry chase. In talking with her mother about the problems in her married life, Molly argued herself around to believing that Dr. P was the very incarnation of evil, a 'sinful man,' a man to whom a promise meant nothing and to whom money was for the spending—spending on what she considered to be frivolities. The more she demanded for the home, the more she insisted that he spend specific hours each day with the children, the more inventive he grew in finding ways to frustrate her. The downward spiral in their marriage was firmly established. Each was altogether unhappy with the other.

When we met him one night at a cocktail party, even the gregarious Dr. P was subdued and had a conspicuous facial tic. After a couple of drinks, he confided to Yvonne that Molly had persuaded her parish priest that the doctor was either possessed or insane. Because attributes of this sort in a physician are hardly conducive to the growth of a healthy practice, he was worried lest these rumors she was putting about as fact would become public knowledge. "It's she who's crazy," he insisted, "she and her damned house! She pays more attention to polishing the floors than she ever did to me. Anyway, this is my last party. I'm going to shape up; otherwise she'll keep on rumor-mongering and divorce me and take off with the children, so I've promised to stay home." Though his sincerity was genuine, somehow his last remark didn't ring true; we didn't think Dr. P would or could live up to his commitment.

Because we are not enthusiastic party-goers ourselves, we didn't observe that Dr. P did in fact keep his word. When next we met him he was a changed man. Gone was the wry smile and the quick joke. Gone was the bright eye; gone the look of even moderate good health. Instead we saw an old, bent man, obviously ill. We proposed to Dr. P that we spend an afternoon with him and Molly, just to see whether we couldn't help in some way. It so happened that we knew of a couple who were precisely the reverse of Dr. P and Molly. In their case, the husband was the home-lover and the wife the gregarious party-going clubwoman. We took this couple with us to the meeting with Molly and Dr. P.

All we really needed to do was sit back and watch the chemistry do its work. The two home-lovers talked about paints and house colors and lawn care; after a very slow start on the part of Dr. P, the two gregarious types were out-punning and out-quipping one another, almost rolling on the floor at their own cleverness, and Dr. P was catching up on the news of his friends among the light society of St. Louis. When this had gone on for some time, we got all four of them to put a rein on their excitement at least long enough to make our point. None of the people present were evil or sinful; none of the people deliberately went out of their way to hurt anyone. It was simply their nature to be the way they were. No exorcism, no threats of sin could change that underlying nature; it could be changed only by dramatic changes in each person's life rhythms: changes which, if not accomplished in the correct manner, could cause ill health.

Molly could see that Dr. P was abruptly improved, even though he had spent only a couple of hours with someone of his own nature. She conceded that she might just have been wrong in her insistence that he be molded to her nature. We hoped and assumed that the understanding she showed in making her admission would bring serenity back into their home.

A couple of months after this meeting, we ourselves moved to a farm some two hours' drive from St. Louis; it wasn't until years later that we learned the final chapter of the story. First the foursome went on a Caribbean vacation together; this was so successful that they started living together. Very soon the two home-lovers, being so much in one another's company, fell in love and divorced their mates.

All this hassle could have been avoided had they only understood before their first marriages what their true natures were and who would make a compatible mate with whom.

Using the Animal in Your Nature

Table I-1 shows the animals which from ancient times have been associated with various birthdates. Even more important, it indicates the areas of life in which each date area will bring strength to you. Later in this book we will get into fine detail on these energies from beyond the stars; but for now the more general strengths will give you all you need so that you can begin using Astromancy to improve your life.

WHAT DO YOU NEED RIGHT NOW?

Serenity? A burst of energy? Whatever it is, look it up in the left column of the table. As an example, let us consider a need for serenity. To gain this, you should take on the attributes of a fish that can swim comfortably in any layer of water and can gain serenity by going down from strong surface waves into the untroubled depths of the sea.

Strengths (the things you gain)	Animal	Birth Date	Ancient Time Period	Symbol
Disrupt friendship Eliminate debts	Phoenix	Jan 20 - Feb 18	Aquarius	♒
Serenity, by adapting to circumstances	Fish	Feb 19 - Mar 20	Pisces	♓
Aggression; bursts of energy	Ram	Mar 21 - Apr 19	Aries	♈
Money through farming or commodities investment	Bull	Apr 20 - May 20	Taurus	♉
Many friendships	Magpie	May 21 - Jun 20	Gemini	♊
Family love	Crab	Jun 21 - Jul 22	Cancer	♋
Friendship and deep loyalty	Lion	Jul 23 - Aug 22	Leo	♌
Green money through retail sales	Virgin maiden	Aug 23 - Sep 22	Virgo	♍
Affectionate love and beauty	Swan	Sep 23 - Oct 22	Libra	♎
A passionate lover	Scorpion	Oct 23 - Nov 21	Scorpio	♏
Luck	Centaur	Nov 22 - Dec 21	Sagittarius	♐
Money through business	Goat	Dec 22 - Jan 19	Capricorn	♑

Table I-1
The Animal in Your Nature

Even more important, you can see from the table what your own natural strengths are. By making your life compatible with those natural strengths, you will avoid much disappointment and illness.

Continuing to read along the Fish/Serenity line, you can see that this month of time has since ancient days been called Pisces.[2] If you were born near the change-over point from one ancient month to the next, you are indeed fortunate; because you will have strengths from both of the months, and through the techniques we will explain, can easily reinforce either strength as it suits your ambitions.

The changes that occur from one sign to the next are gradual. One nature changes imperceptibly to another. Thus if you are born within three or four days of the changeover points of one of the months, you will have the ability readily to assume either identity. These months also have a convenient shorthand in the form of a set of symbols, one representing each of the twelve time periods, as shown in the table.

We cannot emphasize enough how easy it is to assume the nature of another month; or, as we will show later, to use the power of other months to gain your ends. Remember which is the applicable animal; then really concentrate and act out that animal's nature in your daily life; and you will automatically gain all the success you need.

Astromancy in Action

Student File 2G-3XY

Emily D was born in the time period of Scorpio and she exhibited the sexual strength of a scorpion. This meant that she turned most men off because she was very direct when it

---

[2]For convenience we will use the traditional astrological terms for the months of the year. Eventually you should memorize these terms and the animals which represent each one. The ancient months do not tidily correspond to the western Christian calendar months; yet these are the months into which the ancient Watchers divided the years. Astrologers use these months and their ancient names, and so does Ibn Saud.

came to matters of romance—whereas most men like to feel that they, not the woman, are the leader and the conqueror in these matters. In order to lighten up her nature and make her more romantic instead of so forthright, we got her to think of herself as a beautiful swan. Even though Emily was pushing thirty and had thought herself firmly on the shelf, she was soon able to maintain the interest of three or four young men by using her modified nature. In this way she was able to select the one she liked most; she is now happily married to him.

Student File 4Y-2TA

George P was born with the home-loving nature of the crab. He was really over-endowed with this strength. Because he found it almost impossible to get out into the world and make a success of himself, we told him to bring the image of a ram into his life to bring him some of the exploratory aggressive strength of the Aries nature. He took to wearing much brighter colors, and bought himself a red sports car. So abrupt was the change in him that his bosses offered him the position of comptroller of one of their foreign subsidiaries. Quite wisely, George decided to settle for an almost equally important post in his own home town; for although his ram image and his car temporarily changed his nature, still in the long run he would always revert to a crab type; and going overseas would be much too dramatic a change for his nature. Nevertheless because of his brief minor change in nature, George is now a vice-president of the firm and it is fairly certain that he will become president when that position becomes available.

Student File 4Y-6YS

Florence Q, a housewife living in New York, realized that she was driving her family berserk with her fussy nitpicking ways. After analyzing her situation we decided this was because she had the strengths in detail work of her virgin-maiden nature. We advised Florence to try using the magpie image. This easy-going amiable nature allowed her to relax and stop tidying and straightening up and picking at every detail of their apartment and their life. She is still happily using this image every time she finds herself making her family uncomfortable by those natural urges that prompt her to have every detail precisely correct.

Steps to Using Basic Astromancy

As you have already learned, basic Astromancy is simply the assumption for your own use of the strengths you need. Any strength you need is readily available in the basic nature of people born at some specific time of the year. When a child is born into a certain environment, its very first observations of the world imprint it with certain characteristics. In order to get in tune with those characteristics, you should think not only of the animal in the nature but also of the first things a newborn child sees and hears, things that are dependent on the season of birth.

In order to help you magically bring to yourself the nature of another, you need to imagine yourself into the very being of that other nature. You also need to make for yourself amulets for each of the ancient months of the year. Figure I-1 shows a full set of such amulets you can make for yourself. Appendix I to this chapter gives you some thoughts on how a person's nature is modified by the time of year in which he is born. We recommend you use these thoughts to immerse yourself totally in your new personality.

In order to accomplish the personality modification you seek, follow these steps just before that most important date or other event with which you need help.

1. Decide which strength will help you. From Table I-1 find the birthdate, the animal, and the astrological name and symbol that can help you.
2. Place the amulet for that time of year into a small bag of linen or natural cotton. Pin it to an undergarment over your heart, or suspend it around your neck.

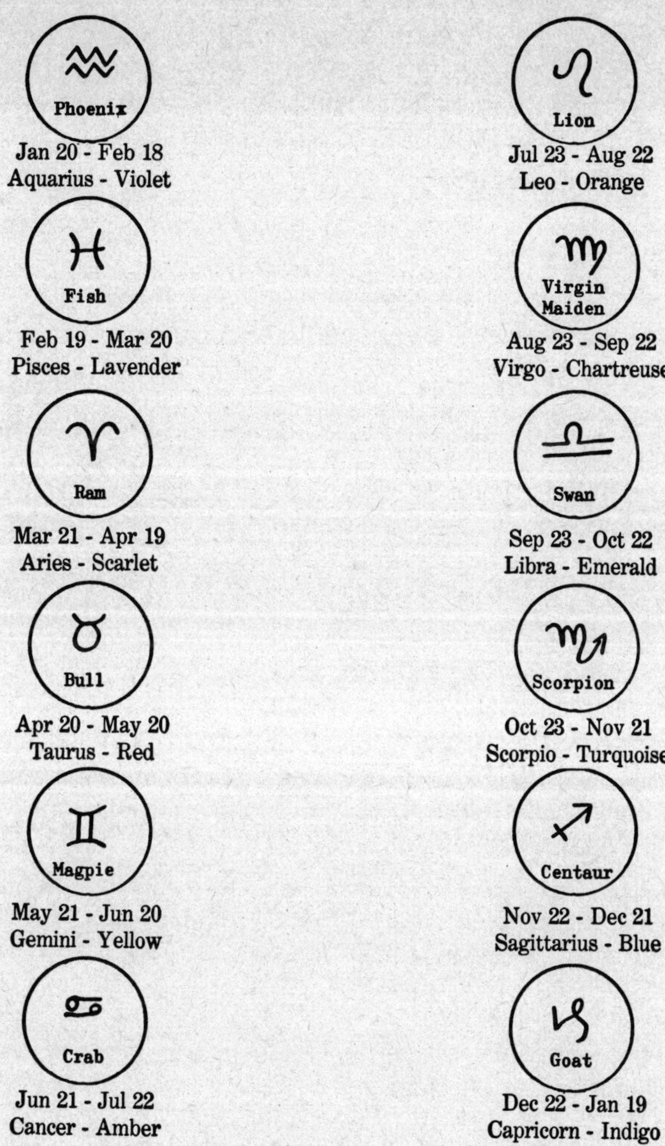

If you find it too expensive to purchase a set of these amulets, copy them on white card and color them as shown.

Figure I-1
Your Own Natural Amulets

3. From the Appendix to this chapter, read the section on the time of year. Read it several times; if possible, commit to memory some key phrases from it.
4. Don't forget to wear clothing of the color appropriate to the time of year.
5. As you approach the situation you wish to control, imagine
    a. the animal and the way it behaves;
    b. the time of year and what it means.

The first time you try Step 5, you may find it difficult; so we recommend for that first attempt you sit quietly at home and do it. Reinforce your new nature every time you feel yourself slipping back or losing the strength you need. You can reinforce anywhere, by visualizing the animal and the time of year in your mind. Many people find that the quiet and privacy of a bathroom is ideal for the reinforcing procedure.

Overcoming All Your Problems

Many people are so weighed down with their problems, and feel so strongly that those problems are insurmountable, that they never attempt to change their nature or their lives. They are almost afraid of change! In most of these cases, using a ram image is all that is needed to shake them loose once and for all from such a defeatist pattern. Most real problems become overwhelming simply because they loom so large in your life that you lose sight of the rest of the world. An effective way of getting your problems in perspective is to use the ram-energy image. Another efficient way is to find someone who is worse off than yourself, and help him out of his difficulties. There are newspaper stories every day of people who have suffered birth defects or accidents, but through sheer willpower have recovered and made new lives for themselves. Often these lives are better than the life they led before their loss. The handicap shook them loose from their humdrum life. Because of it, they had to be exposed to new situations and new people; they found new strengths in their natures which allowed them to succeed where they might otherwise have been failures. Probably one of the most inspiring multiple-amputees in history is the present head of the Veterans' Administration, Max Cleland. Here is a man with only one arm and no legs—who heads a major government agency. What would you think of life if you were suddenly to lose both your legs and most of one arm? Wouldn't that make you worse off than you are right now? By helping others, and by seeing how those who are worse off than you have succeeded, you get your own problems into perspective and can Astromantically deal with them one at a time, selecting each time the nature you need to use to overcome most easily that specific problem. Probably the only real handicap you must combat and conquer is a certain lack of strengths implicit in the date of your birth. Isn't it better if you start now to improve your life than if you wait for some catastrophe to hit you?

Lover, Millionaire, Warrior: Any Nature You Need Can Be Yours

When Ibn Saud revealed to us from beyond the grave the secret of using the strengths of the natures of people born in various months to gain anything that was desired, the principle appeared to be so simple and so obvious that we promptly began testing it. As a result of those tests, we can assure you that you can have the financial and business strength of someone born in the month of Capricorn (the Goat), or the romantic strength of someone born in the month of Libra (the Swan), or in fact the strengths of any of the time segments, easily and quickly at your command. All it takes is for you to use the imagining technique we have given you, and you can instantly add to your present strength the strength of another birthdate.

We were skeptical that those added strengths could be made to last long enough actually to change a life. Again, however, tests have shown that the wise sage knew whereof he spoke; for hundreds of people have changed their natures using his methods, and have made new lives for themselves using the techniques he taught us from beyond the grave.

Chapter I—Appendix I

THE IMAGE STRENGTHS OF VARIOUS BIRTHDATES

Strength	Animal	Birthdate	Calendar Name
Disrupt Friendships Eliminate Debts	Phoenix	Jan 21 – Feb 21	Aquarius

The Phoenix is a mythical bird that rises from its own ashes. This image of flying free after burning your bridges is the basic strength of this birthdate period. Last year is gone, and a new year is beginning.

Midwinter is here, when the light blue sky and the dark of night combine to give a violet hue. It is time to invent games to beguile the idle hours. New ideas, new ways, new things, all must be used to keep boredom from the door. The friends around the fire will follow your new ideas. The Aquarius is quick-witted, always exploring new things. From his exploration he attracts a group of interesting friends who often apply new ways of doing old things, thus pushing outward the frontiers of knowledge and gaining much success. Violet is the color that best expresses these new ways. It is not by chance that groups experimenting with new life-styles use violet in their color schemes, for this is their natural hue.

Strength	Animal	Birthdate	Calendar Name
Serenity, through Adapting to Circumstances	Fish	Feb 22 – Mar 21	Pisces

The Fish swims unnoticed in many different waters: in the calm shallows or deeper, out of harm's way. When the water is rough, Pisces behaves like a fish, drifting and swimming with the water.

Spring is almost here, but still you have to wait for its green mantle. While you wait for spring to burst into flower, you remind yourself that it is your time of year. The long indigo nights and blue skies begin to pale into lavender, the color of spring's mysterious time.

Patience is often said to be a virtue; and when things require time to ripen, this is the nature with which you can wait patiently for the first new shoots of spring. You can make yourself small and invisible in a crowd by wearing pale, watery colors. Like a fish, you swim in and out between other fishes, not touching them, hardly affecting them; but because you know the cycle will come round, you will be successful through patience.

Strength	Animal	Birthdate	Calendar Name
Agression Burst of Energy	Ram	Mar 21 – Apr 20	Aries

The Ram, ancient symbol of spring energy and fertility, is the animal to be emulated when you seek to gain the courage and energy to explore your environment and lead the goats to safety. As the days grow longer and warmer, it is time to begin all those projects you have been postponing, to get out and explore new territories. Start new friendships now, when everyone feels the lift of spring in the air. The blood flows swiftly in the spring, and that blood-flow is symbolized by red. Because of the possible negative connotations of red, you must be wary of wearing too much red, especially if you are a man, when you wish to put the Aries strength into your life; but you can easily bring in a red beanbag chair and red foods such as pizza and other hotly spiced Italian dishes. If you can afford it, a new red car will energize Aries, or a new paint job on the old one. The ram-red combination reminds you of the swiftly flowing heat of the blood and will encourage you to get out and explore.

Strength	Animal	Birthdate	Calendar Name
Money through Farming or Commodities Investment	Bull	Apr 21 – May 21	Taurus

The Bull stands firm against adversity. He has his feet planted in the rich earth; he gains his strength from contact with the earth and through such things as dealing in the produce commodity markets.

In the Tauran month, the earth is plowed and seeds are planted. The stubbornness, the persistence of this hard work is typical of the strength of the Taurus. It is a long haul between the sowing of the seeds and the reaping of the harvest. When the crop is sown, solid wealth is in the ground, and the Taurus energy gives persistence and strength that will guard the crop until it is harvested.

Strength	Animal	Birthdate	Calendar Name
Make Friends Easily	Magpie	May 22 – Jun 21	Gemini

The Magpie is a friendly bird, always chattering and flitting about. It seeks objects that glitter but are light enough to be carried off to the nest. You can distract with magpie chatter so that you too can carry away your prize. You can beguile away the lengthening days with jokes and quick turns of phrase.

The seeds are in the ground; yellow blossoms abound. The quick darting flight of the magpie is your natural gift. This is another season of waiting. The wait for the seeds to germinate and bear fruit requires use of your high mental activity to help the slower people with jokes and entertainment. Your light attitude to life allows you to get through the most difficult situations without harm. When things are badly awry in your life, it is good to take the strengths of Gemini; for by becoming a Gemini you will not be affected by heavy problems. The light yellow of blossoms is your natural color, as the flight of the magpie demonstrates your behavior pattern.

Strength	Animal	Birthdate	Calendar Name
Family Love	Crab	Jun 22 – Jul 22	Cancer

The Crab has a secure home under the rocks where none can reach him. He always approaches problems walking sideways, looking them over, never showing the opponent exactly what it is he wants. In this month the first fruits begin to ripen, and bringing the harvest home to the family hearth is the Crab's concern. Firm, safe relationships are cemented in your comfortable home. The long wait is over; the harvest is beginning. Your color is the amber of the ripening corn; it signals the security that will be born of a well-stocked and -tended home base. In this nature you can find a lifetime friend or mate, one who will always be at your side to share the harvest and your bed and board.

Strength	Animal	Birthdate	Calendar Name
Friendship and Loyalty	Lion	Jul 23 – Aug 22	Leo

Because they are so strong and invincible, lions don't have to prove anything to anyone. They are powerful but friendly; for they know that if attacked, they will always win—as you will when you use this image.

The sun is high, shining on the golden corn of the harvest. There is plenty for all, and it can be shared; for from this golden time of year you gain the strengths you need always to win. Because you know with confidence that you need not prove yourself, you never need to be cunning or manipulative.

Anyone who looks can see the wealth of the harvest and the strength of the lion. That strength implies loyalty to friends.

Strength	Animal	Birthdate	Calendar Name
Green Money through Retail Sales	Virgin Maiden	Aug 23 – Sep 22	Virgo

The virgin maid is quiet, shy, and retiring. She needs help, and all will try to help her; in this way she gains much cash. She is careful, prim, and proper, even though underneath she knows she can influence anyone to help her. Her careful work in the fields makes her kill every insect, collect every grain; these small details make the difference between an ordinary harvest and a bounteous one. The new grass peeps from among the cornstalks, giving an unusual mixed chartreuse as the color for this season of the year.

Strength	Animal	Birthdate	Calendar Name
Affectionate Love and Beauty	Swan	Sep 23 – Oct 22	Libra

The Swan glides on the lake, the very essence of beauty and serenity. This is a relaxed time of year, when the crops are coming in and food is plentiful. In this season the abundance of nature is everywhere to be seen.

After the hot summer, cool nights are coming in, nights meant for romance. Yellows and greens are appropriate to this time of year; to key your senses further to the Swan, you should wear them; not the lighter tints of springtime, but the dark greens and dark yellows of harvest.

Strength	Animal	Birthdate	Calendar Name
Passionate Lover	Scorpion	Oct 23 – Nov 21	Scorpio

The Scorpion is full of energy; when in good health, it is constantly copulating with its mates. But beware, for the

Scorpion has a deadly sting that comes from an unexpected direction. Occasionally the Scorpion stings even the thing he loves best—or himself.

This is the hunting time of year. That fact gives the Scorpio a nature with marked singleness of purpose, combined with a hunter's cunning that means the eventual objective will be obtained. The objective must be obtained; for if it is not, the tribe will not eat. The intimate connection between birth and death makes the Scorpio wish to replace all that is killed; consequently a heavy drive to procreate is inherent in his nature. The browns of the autumn woodland are the Scorpio's protective coloration.

Strength	Animal	Birthdate	Calendar Name
Luck	Centaur	Nov 22 – Dec 21	Sagittarius

The horse with the archer's head combines the power and lovability of the horse with some of the hunter's directness of purpose. This again is a powerful, self-possessed, easy-going type, a type which nothing daunts. They have innumerable friends whose shortcomings are readily forgiven. The Centaur expects nothing of anyone and is friendly with everyone. Good cheer, good ale, good food, all in abundance are characteristic of this season. The blue of the sky on a clear winter's day is your color, a color that makes you think of friends and good companions.

Strength	Animal	Birthdate	Calendar Name
Money through Business	Goat	Dec 22 – Jan 20	Capricorn

The Goat succeeds through its ability to eat and absorb anything. Whatever is left over, you can convert to wealth. In business affairs, you make sure that waste is minimized; thus you are always successful.

The dark blue velvet sky of long winter nights is yours. This is the most serious time of year; in its image you will be able to impress business associates, especially bankers. The dark blue business suit is ideal for this serious, solid citizen, who wants—and gets—his rights. If the fellow down the block gets a loan, with this nature you too will get a loan or know the reason why. Remember: You are watching the winter food store, making sure everything gets equally divided.

Chapter Two

POWERING YOUR WHEEL OF ASTROMANTIC FORTUNE

What This Chapter Will Do for You

"The unplanned life is not worth living." That saying is as true now as it was when it was first uttered in ancient Greece. Therefore this chapter will:

- Give you a basic understanding of the seven-year cycles in your life
- Show you how to adjust those cycles to maximize your successes
- Show you how to divine and power your life so that it is better in all its facets
- Teach you to use this same technique to power and adjust the lives of those around you

Understanding Thy Life Cycles

Even the dullest-witted can easily see that thy life is divided naturally into rhythmic cycles, each lasting seven years. Just as the month of thy birth affects thy nature, even so the period of thy life which thou art inhabiting affects thy development and success. Allah in His wisdom decreed that every seven years thou shouldst find thyself in a different state of thy life. Reflect for a moment. Thy first seven years, thou wert tied to thy mother. Then thou didst enter school. At the age of 14, thou didst enter early manhood or womanhood: what in thy time they call 'puberty.' At the age of 21, thou didst reach a man's estate and at 28 thou art leading a family. In my time as it is in thine, a man who is worth anything doth begin a new career in his 35th year . . . And thus the seven-year cycle repeateth itself. These various ages can be called Preparation, Work, Mastery, and Leadership. Knowing that these phases exist in thy life, thou canst either abide by the rules that Allah in His wisdom laid down; or thou canst progress more rapidly around the spiral by condensing thy life as I will instruct thee. The one thing thou canst not do is ignore the effect of these phases on thy life; for if thou dost ignore them, thou art railing and fighting against that which is as immutable as the very stars in the heavens. Thou canst not ignore them; for they affect every living creature on this planet.

Ed B Adjusts His Life Cycle

Student File 2Y-OGL

Ed was the president of a small electronics firm in Southern California, one that he had built up laboriously over seven years of hard work. Although he was president of the company, he was not the majority shareholder, and he was distraught when the firm was sold to a nationwide conglomerate. Ed had had an interest in the electrical energy emanating from animals; and because of this we had had many conversations with him. When we told him that he should rest on his laurels because he was now in a Preparation phase of his life, he laughed at us. He was not content to let it go at that, however; he wanted to break the long-term seven-year cycle of his life by sheer resistance—and he failed.

After spending a couple of years and most of his savings in futile attempts to get back into management of an electronics company, he began to believe us. His life was a wreck. With little or no money left, he agreed to follow the steps we suggested. Ed was the first subject on whom we tried Ibn Saud's system to accelerate the long cycles. He decided to add a whole 14 years to his life cycle with the technique.

Again, as with the technique for changing your nature, the seven-year cycle technique was dramatically successful. Ed founded a new firm and very soon was producing a computer terminal for a whole new generation of equipment. This time he retained control of his company; when he was approached once more by the same conglomerate that had bought his previous business out from under him, he was able not only to make a good deal financially, but also to obtain the position of vice-president in charge of all research for the conglomerate, a position which dovetailed perfectly with the Mastery phase to which he had accelerated himself. He enjoys that position to this day.

Using the Cycles of Your Life

Figure II-1 shows a life-cycle dial. Look at your present age to see what you can expect, both currently and in the near future. As you move around the left-hand side of the dial, clearly your income will increase; as you move around its right-hand side, your income will normally decrease. If this situation is not satisfactory to you, you may wish to move rapidly around the dial to another point on it as Ed did, so that you can change your long cycle from one of Preparation, for example, to one of Leadership. Alternatively, you may wish to wait and prepare yourself for the new phase of your life as it comes around in due course.

As you will learn in Chapter III, you are exposed to every sort of energy from the heavens not just once a year,

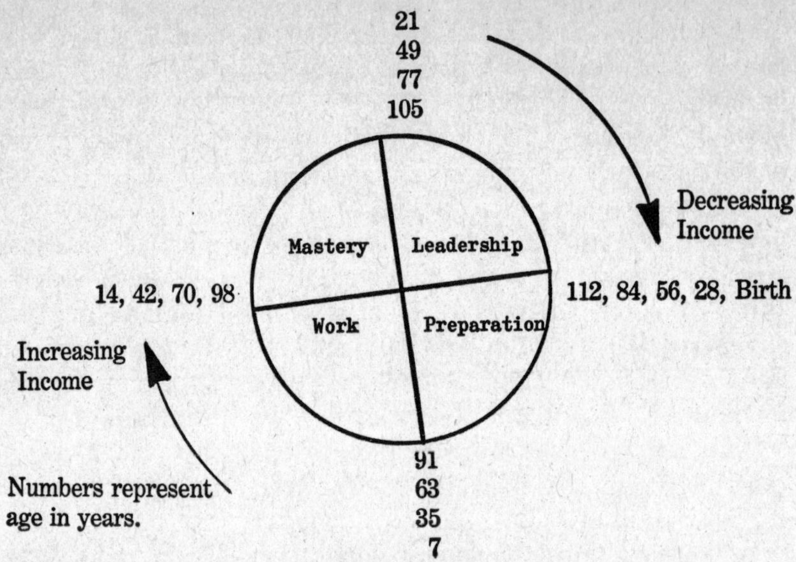

Figure II-1
Your Life Cycle Dial

but once in each 24-hour period. This is the basic reason that astrologers are able to predict your life by making each day equivalent to a year. In Ibn Saud's technique for adjusting the seven-year cycle, he does the same thing: Each year is made equivalent to one day. Thus if you wish to accelerate your seven-year cycle by fourteen years, you must follow the technique for fourteen days; that is, for two complete seven-year cycles. The technique requires that you go to a quiet place where you will not be under any pressure, for the number of days equivalent to the number of years you wish to progress your cycles. Within the number of days that you have decided upon, you must follow strictly the following regimen:

1. For the first three days you must stay in one room, preferably without clothing (although a simple robe of white cotton does not seem to interfere with the process) and fast, eating only bread and honey, and drinking only water to which honey and vinegar have been added in the proportion of one teaspoon each to a glass of water.

2. As the second phase, you must spend a day in total meditation and withdrawal. During this day, nothing of the mundane life should be allowed to intrude upon your awareness.

3. In the next three days, you may come back into the world again, eating and drinking anything you wish. At the end of this three-day cycle, when you are totally "up," you should purchase a terrestrial globe, one which is capable of being spun on its axis.

4. Sit now and turn the globe the number of revolutions that represents the years you have progressed. As you turn the globe, carefully see yourself spiritually and magically aging and entering the phase of the seven-year cycle that you desire. You can see this phase as the next turn upward in the spiral; Figure II-2 shows the life spiral in diagrammatic form.

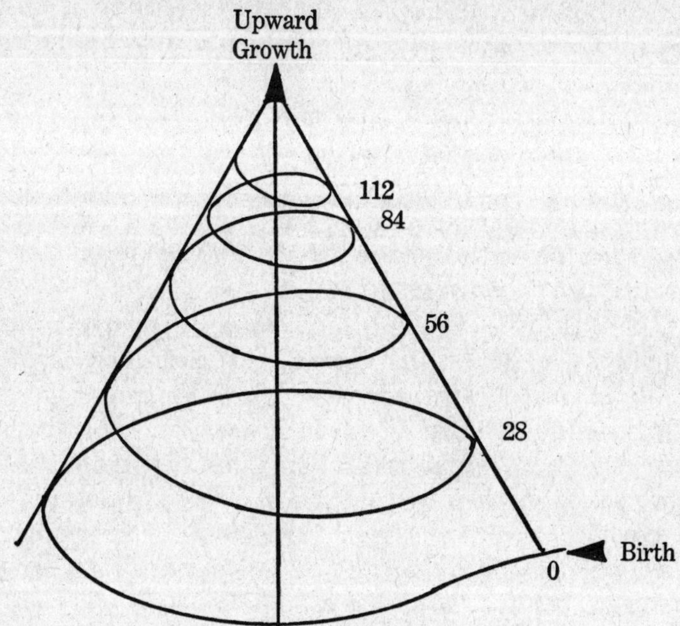

Each phase is higher and better than the one before.

Figure II-2
Your Life Spiral

Dynamic Living

As I look down the centuries at the wonders of the modern world, I say unto thee: The only thing that hath not changed is the nature of human beings. Still I see the lethargy of the man who hath enough in his belly. Still I see the violence of youth, the fiery love affairs, and still I see the follies of the leaders and the young nations who in the vigor of the spring of their life do commit grievous crimes against their neighbors. I say unto thee that this is not the way to happiness and serenity. If thy belly were less full, thou wouldst strive mightily; thou wouldst not sit as thou dost when thou art passing the wastes from thy body, waiting hopefully for others to do thy work and to make thy life more serene. Change thy life. Get out as thy forefathers did. Rise up and succeed. Instead of sleeping this day away, wreak some change. Just as the wind doth change the shape of the desert by moving one grain of sand at a time, thou canst change thy life by taking one step at a time toward the bountiful rewards thou canst and shouldst have.

If thou hast not the energy to follow my simple advice, then I say unto thee: Thou dost not deserve happiness and success; for the techniques that I prescribe can make thy life bountiful, yet they are as simple as a rosebud.

The first thing thou must do is establish what is amiss in thy present life. Since time began, man hath recognized that it is his innermost nature that doth first need attention; and that proceeding outward from this nature, all other things do follow in natural sequence. When thou hast diagnosed the strengths and the needs of thine own nature, then and only then canst thou progress to diagnosing the strengths and needs of thy body; and then and only then canst thou progress to the relationships thou hast established with other entities on thy plane. This progressive sequence hath been known since the ancient time when the Watchers were set to study the heavenly Wheel. It is not some great unknown thing—yet it is today a great magical secret, one which I freely divulge to thee for thy use and betterment.

Claire Awakens Herself

Student File 4G-4ND

Claire D, a former resident of Montreal, has many psychic gifts. In the privacy of her own home, for instance, she could change the color of a candle flame; and she could get her husband Bill to call her on the telephone just by projecting the thought that she wanted badly to hear from him. Again and again we urged Claire to get out and demonstrate her gifts to other people, but somehow she never would.

The only cause of discontent in Claire's life was her wish for a Bahamas island retreat where she could get away from the cold of Montreal and its cramped apartment style of life. She was forever harping on this subject to Bill, much to the detriment of their otherwise placid and friendly relationship. Claire literally made herself sick by constantly worrying about how she was going to get the money to fulfill her dream. She tried her psychic gifts against the lottery, but she found (as many have before her) that when you are emotionally involved in something your psychic gifts become blocked. She insisted she ought to win a million dollars in one windfall; she spent all the family's spare money on little schemes to fulfill her desire. She cut down on the grocery budget; she refused to pay even for repair of the TV set; she would not go out to dinner or to a movie. All the money she saved in these ways she lost by playing the lottery and gambling in other ways.

We warned her over and over that this obsession with money and the Big Win would make her ill, and indeed it did. After a bout with a psychologist she reluctantly gave up her dream and resigned herself to what she saw as a small, humdrum life of drudgery in Montreal. Instead of the vivacious and interesting woman she had been, she now became a drab, sullen, embittered harridan. Bill disliked intensely this aspect of Claire which had been brought out by the psychologist; he would even have been glad for a return of the hectic times before. He started to seek serenity and companionship outside their home. Seeing this, Claire felt that life without her Bahamian paradise and without her husband was not worth living, and tried to commit suicide. This landed her in the hands of another psychiatrist—but this one, like Claire herself, was a student of our School. He told her that the sudden change that had been forced on her nature was making her psychopathic, and that abrupt changes of this type were always traumatic. He pointed out to her that her dream of a Bahamas hideaway could be fulfilled, but that her first task must now be to get her nature back in tune with reality. When this was done, then she could proceed to reestablishing relationships with her husband and her former friends. *Then* she could begin to accumulate money for her dream in a balanced way; not in the way she previously had, by trying to do it all at once, but doing a little at a time. He fell back on our old suggestion that she should teach psychic development classes, thereby earning a modest income which she could gradually build toward her dream retreat.

Her classes were immediately successful, especially among businessmen; for the method she taught them to use in the prediction of business deals saved them hundreds of thousands, if not millions, of dollars. In gratitude one of the businessmen allowed her the use of his company's plane to fly to the Bahamas and spend two weeks at one of the resort hotels.

She did not like it. Her dream had been based on TV and movie fantasies. She found the town too hot, too dirty, too smelly, and too expensive for her liking. Of course she did not visit any of the beautiful out-islands, but spent her vacation in Nassau, which after all is a busy port and tourist city, not a place to learn of the real island life. Nevertheless, when Claire came back to Canada, she no longer wanted to live in the Bahamas. Instead, after some rational discussions with Bill, they moved to a farm just outside Vancouver. In this milder climate she is a contented and relaxed lady. If she has not achieved her original goal, she has at least gained total balanced happiness and serenity.

Diagnosing Your Life's Path with a Wheel of Growth

Ibn Saud pointed out to us that we must progressively, in a balanced way, review and correct any insufficiencies we may have in our life. Figure II-3 shows the wheel of progressive growth in your life. Begin first by considering your inborn nature. As you progress in a clockwise direction around the wheel, you see that the wheel guides you outward from your nature into other, more worldly, aspects of experience. Take the twelve symbol disks that you made for the work of changing your nature in Chapter I, and lay them out before you on a table with an enlarged copy of the chart in Figure II-3. Now consider each of the segments in turn. In order to do this, consider first your inner nature. Take the three disks which represent the energies that you would most like to bring into your nature, and place them face upward below your drawing of the wheel of growth. Now close your eyes. Place your left hand on the segment of the wheel of growth that you are considering, and with your right hand feel the energy flowing from each of the three disks you have selected.[1] You will feel that one of the disks gives more energy than the other two. Take that high-energy disk and place it on the first segment of your wheel of growth. Repeat this procedure for each succeeding segment of the wheel. As you progress toward the end, you will find that the symbol disks fall naturally into the remaining segments. Of course you could use several disks all having the same symbol on them, but this would not give you a balanced result. The idea in using the twelve disks and matching them to the twelve segments is that when you have completed the diagram you will have a balanced life diagnosis.

Now by simply looking at the wheel of growth, you can see which symbol disk you should use in every single one of your life's endeavors.

---

[1]If you are left-handed, reverse these directions.

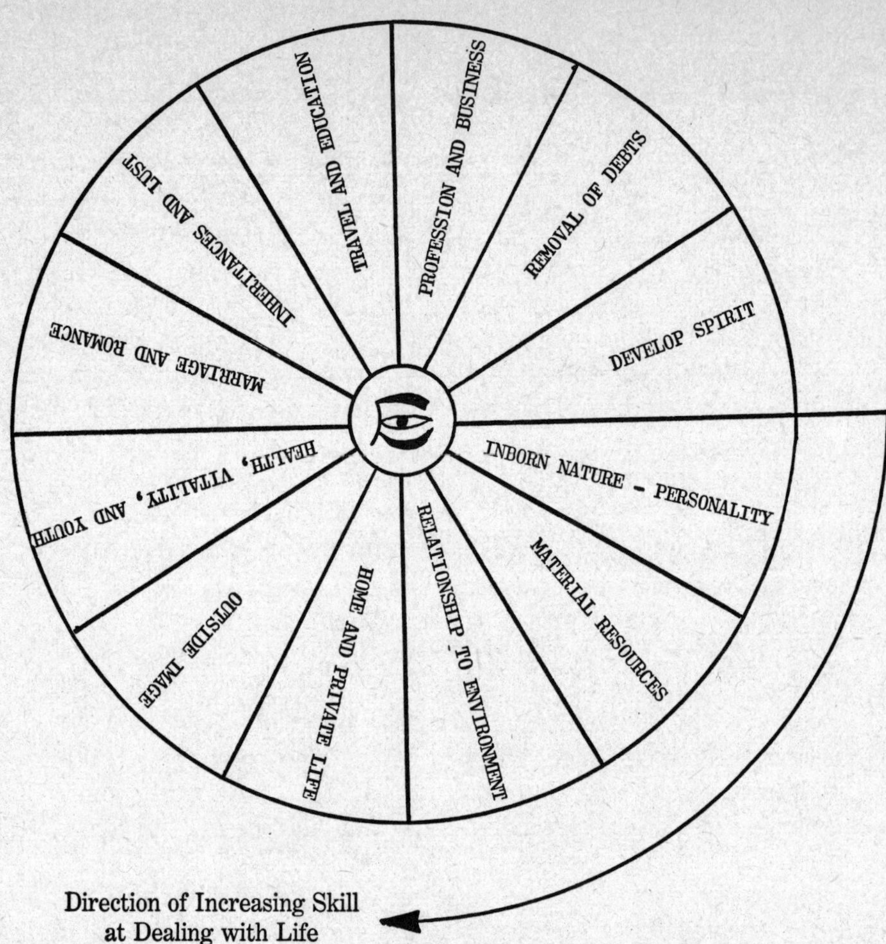

Figure II-3
Wheel of Progressive Growth

Fulfilling the Potential of Thy Life

Verily I say unto thee: This day could be thy last. How wouldst thou wish to be remembered by thy friends? As a whining lazy do-nothing person? Or as someone who hath trodden the sands of foreign shores and lived life to its fullest? It is in thy hands, for thou canst change thy nature as easily as thou dost change thy robe. Once in exhorting his troops to battle a great English king did say,

In peace there's nothing so becomes a man
As modest stillness and humility;
But when the blast of war blows in our ears,
Then imitate the action of the tiger;
Stiffen the sinews, summon up the blood,
Disguise fair nature with hard-favour'd rage:
Then lend the eye a terrible aspect;
Let it pry through the portage of the head
Like the brass cannon; let the brow o'erwhelm it
As fearfully as doth a galled rock
O'erhang and jutty his confounded base,
Swill'd with the wild and wasteful ocean.
Now set the teeth, and stretch the nostril wide;
Hold hard the breath, and bend up every spirit!

Thou as well canst also put on the visage of any nature thou desirest. Thou canst wear the visage of the lion and canst demand thy rights from the lowly bazaar-keeper or government scribe; and behold, when thou puttest on this visage thou wilt get what thou deservest and requirest.

Learn thou well the strengths of the twelve animals in nature. Imagine thyself into their visage and their bodies, and thou wilt indeed gather unto thyself their strengths and natural characteristics. Mayhap thou hast had a prophet foretell thy future for thee. Mayhap this hath even been done with the aid of thy birthdate and mayhap a chart hath been drawn. What didst thou do with it? Didst thou merely read it and feel amused, and then lay it aside? Or didst thou use it? Or change it by changing thy nature, so that the dread predictions could be avoided and the happy predictions be enhanced? It is thy very life thou art considering. Art thou going to live it like a stone under the sands of the desert? Or art thou going to emerge from the grave thou hast made for thyself, and change thy life so that thy friends admire thee and talk of thy success? If truly today should be thy last day, what wouldst thou be remembered for?

Widow Jenkins Regains Her Fortune

Student File 6G-1VA

Mrs. Jenkins became a widow on her 62nd birthday. She and Herb had been out to a good restaurant near their home in London, and he had choked to death on a bite of steak. This terribly shocking experience, seeing her husband strangle before her very eyes, added enormously to the trauma of Mrs. Jenkins as she changed abruptly from the married to the widowed state.

By nature Mrs. Jenkins was a Swan, very relaxed and romantically inclined. With Herb's insurance money she decided she would take a trip around the world to fulfill her need for romantic adventure. She met and married Earnest, who was somewhat younger than herself. She was content to place all her affairs in the hands of her new husband as she had in Herb's. As you might guess, this folly resulted in Earnest's stripping her accounts and absconding with most of her money. Of course we believe that all this occurred because Mrs. Jenkins was still traumatized by Herb's death, and in this condition she allowed her Swan nature full range.

We had been corresponding with Mrs. Jenkins for several years, and in her time of trouble she turned to us for solace and advice. She used Ibn Saud's technique to enhance the bull-like aspect of her nature and turn the rest of her personality toward more persistence. She vowed never to rest until she had tracked Earnest down and brought him to justice.

Remembering the way Earnest had found her on a cruise ship, Mrs. Jenkins scanned the passenger lists of the various cruise liners. Sure enough, she found him on a ship that was due to transit the Panama Canal the following week and then sail up the west coast of the Americas, calling at Acapulco and then Los Angeles. Promptly she contacted the boat's agents and learned that some space was still available. Using her credit cards, she was able to fly out to Panama and catch the ship when it docked in Colon. She quickly learned that Earnest was deeply involved with another woman who, she discovered from the purser, was Mrs. S, heiress to a multimillion-dollar fortune.

When the ship had transited the Canal and was safely out to sea past Balboa, Mrs. Jenkins approached Earnest. He soon recovered from his initial shock and tried to bluster his way out of his actions. When this failed, he tried to reawaken the romance. With her adjusted personality traits, Mrs. Jenkins was having none of that. She laid it on the line: "Give me back my money or I'll queer your pitch with Mrs. S. And while I'm thinking about it, duck, let's get divorced in Acapulco; you can give me 50,000 pounds as my divorce settlement." Feeling confident of his control over Mrs. S, Earnest readily agreed to her proposal. When the ship anchored for a four-day stay at Acapulco, Earnest pretended to be ill. He and Mrs. Jenkins went ashore in a ship's boat. Earnest transferred from his Bahamas account the money of which he had defrauded Mrs. Jenkins as well as the 50,000 pounds for her settlement. Then they arranged their 24-hour divorce.

On their return to the ship, Mrs. Jenkins radiotelephoned her bank in England, telling them to contact her as soon as the money was safely deposited. By the time she received that confirmation, the ship was about to dock in Los Angeles. She had the ship's radio operator photostat both her marriage certificate and her divorce certificate. Her last act in her adjusted identity before she packed her bag and left was to seal these two photostats in an envelope and leave them for the purser to deliver to Mrs. S, a thing she would never have dreamed of doing if she had been her old happy-go-lucky self.

Using Your Outreach Personality Tuner

The diagnostic wheel of growth that you used earlier in this chapter can also be used to enhance various aspects of your relationships with the world around you. Mrs. Jenkins used the wheel to change her basic personality, her attitude to money, and her attitude to marriage so that she could deal with Earnest with these character attributes newly strengthened. When you are going into any particularly difficult situation in your life, you should re-examine your wheel of growth and select from it those interface areas where modification will help you achieve the end you desire. In Mrs. Jenkins' case, she placed the Bull disk on Personality so that she could have the strength of personality of the Bull to carry forward her plans. She wanted to get her money back so she placed on the Money segment her Lion disk, which meant she would gain gold. In the marriage area she wished not to be affected by Earnest, so there she placed the light-hearted Magpie. She did not bother to place any disks in other areas because she did not feel that the other interfaces were relevant to her problem.

You may find that in your own case many areas of your life need adjustment if you are to reach out and gain your full potential. To use the disks yourself, you need only think about the situation that you are going to go into and decide which interface areas need changing; then select from your symbol disks the appropriate animal natures that will allow you to fulfill your desires. Place them on the chart close to the center when you need a minor modification or enhancement of strength, and close to the outside rim when you need major extra strengths in your life. Figure II-4 shows the chart which Mrs. Jenkins carried with her during the time she spent successfully resolving her problems with Earnest.

Using the Natural Strengths and Weaknesses of Others

Thou mayest think that the sheik or emir hath more strength than thou hast; but I say unto thee verily that this is a crooked way of thinking. In most cases the sheik or emir was born unto his wealth or he did gain his riches and position with the aid of pure chance. Yea, it may be true that the

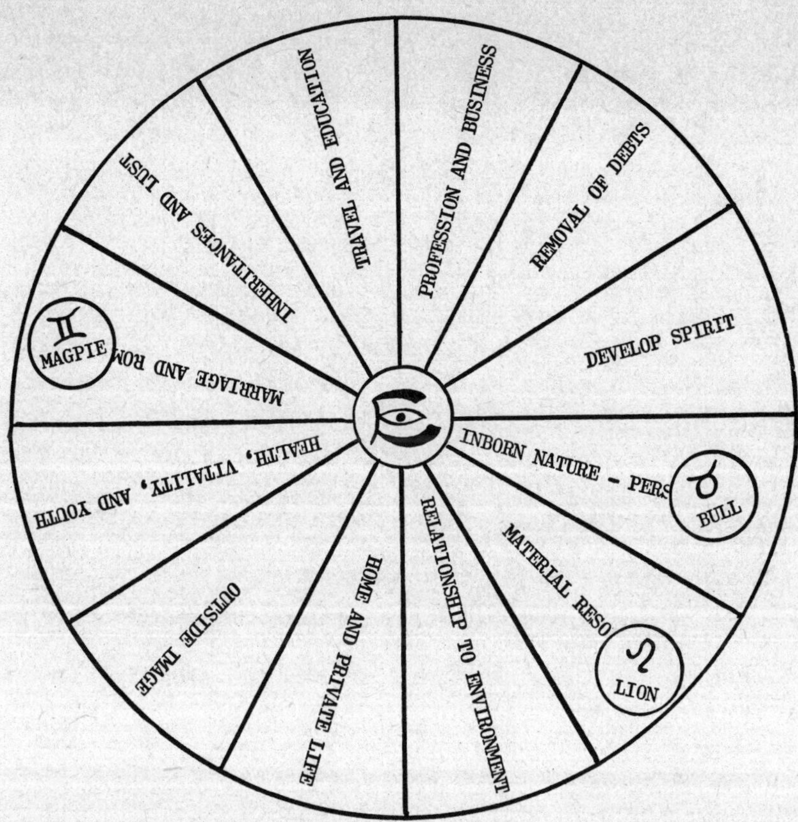

Move animal disks closer to center for less influence.

Figure II-4
Mrs. Jenkins' Winning Chart

sheik hath certain character strengths which thou lackest—but thou in thy turn hast character strengths which he lacketh. Because thou hast lived a hard life, it is most assuredly true that thou hast stronger fiber than the man who hath been coddled since the cradle in the lap of luxury. In my time as in thy time, we have seen the corruption of the mighty—corruption which taketh place when their weaknesses are exploited by the silent jackals of the desert who control and manipulate the so-called leaders of our peoples for their own ends. I say unto thee that all men have strengths and weaknesses; and when all thine individual strengths and weaknesses are added together, the sum will come out larger than the sum of the strengths and weaknesses of many of thy so-called 'betters.'

Thou too canst be like unto the jackal of the desert, living on thy wits. Thou canst use the strengths and weaknesses of thine adversaries to thine advantage; for through knowledge of a person's nature thou canst control him. Invite thine enemy into thy house. Put on the face of friendship. Diagnose for him his life, using the wheel of growth that I have shown thee. When thou hast done this, thou wilt know thine enemy.

The Russians Get the United States' Most Vital Secrets

Time and again Ibn Saud's words have proven true. The recent Korean influence-buying scandal in Washington DC is only one example of how the weaknesses of our government leaders were exploited and their strengths in office perverted to the advantage of South Korea.

An agent is recruited because of character weaknesses—weaknesses in the sexual, greed, drug, gambling, or other areas. Through the ages, with disquieting frequency, prominent men have been turned into traitors through exploitation of their weaknesses. Once he has been made an agent, the man's strengths are used to accomplish the controller's purpose. You probably know of many cases. One that seems to have been hushed up is the story of a sergeant in the United States Army.

Sergeant M had the characteristic strong-lion traits—but he also had the Lion's weakness of failing to comprehend when other people lied to him or did cunning and crooked things to him. The Russian intelligence agency, the KGB, were thus able to get him in their clutches. It all started when other people were promoted around Sergeant M and another man got the job in Berlin for which the Sergeant had been hoping for many years. He was deeply discouraged and suffered a lengthy period of depression. During this time Sergeant M's girlfriend Heidi introduced him to KGB agents. First they asked him for what seemed to be only innocuous information; gradually, between his fondness for Heidi and his honesty—for he believed that the KGB agents were actually CIA agents assigned to check office security—he gave them more and more information. Years went by. Sergeant M married Heidi, got out of the Army, and took a civilian job in Las Vegas. Again he was approached by the KGB. They threatened to expose his part in the earlier espionage unless he reenlisted in the Army and resumed providing them with the information they wanted. Sergeant M realized that he had been tricked; but over the years his bitterness and disillusion had caused him to become more loyal to Heidi and her communist ideas than to the United States. So he did as the KGB asked. Eventually he was put in charge of the vault near Paris where all United States top-secret documents were held before their distribution to American commanders in Europe. With the aid of KGB equipment, he was able to crack the vault and photograph the documents. As time went by he was promoted away from that position, back to Washington; thus the flow of information to the Communists ceased.

Sergeant M began to go off on prolonged drinking binges, perhaps to assuage his conscience. During one of these, Heidi was questioned by FBI agents and confessed to the espionage in which she had collaborated. Sergeant M pleaded guilty and drew the maximum 25-year sentence for his crimes. Pentagon officials stated these crimes cost the United States millions of dollars because American codes and code equipment had to be redesigned and many strategic plans had to be revised.

Diagnosing and Powering Those around You to New Lives

Although we have been discussing the negative aspects of controlling others and getting the things you wish from them, of course there is a positive aspect as well to this facet of Astromancy. You may find in your life's path an obstacle in the form of a person who is too lethargic to help himself. If this person could be made to get off the dime, oftentimes your own path would be easier. Many times relatives assume they require all your attention—when in fact all they are doing is depending on you for things they could do themselves. In such a case, take an Astromantic personality chart and place *their* name or their picture at the top of it. Then place on it symbol disks that will make these people move in the direction you wish; that is, enhance the aspects of their personality that will bring self-reliance, wealth, lovers, whatever is required, into their life. In this way you can get out from under the burden they represent, and will be free to proceed along your path more easily.

Putting the Knowledge of This Chapter to Use in Your Life

Every journey to a better life has to have a beginning. We recommend that you make that beginning *today* by learning which of the seven-year cycles you are actually in and deciding whether or not that is the *correct* cycle for the life plan you have formulated for yourself. For instance: If at this stage of your life plan you are trying to be a successful leader but you are not in a leadership phase, then the first thing you must do is adjust your life phasing as described in the early pages of this chapter.

Having adjusted your life phasing, you can diagnose for yourself your life's new path and establish which strengths you need to enhance for achievement of your long-term goals. As you progress along your path, occasionally you will have particular obstacles to overcome. These are the times when you should use your Astromancy personality chart to tune your interfaces with the world so that you can maximize your appropriate strengths.

People nowadays are so willing to talk about their birthdates and what their birth sign means that it is child's play to get them to agree to your 'doing a reading' for them. In this way you can penetrate their innermost nature, learning what their weaknesses are and what strengths you can reach through those weaknesses.

Chapter Three

YOUR PLACE IN THE COSMIC CYCLE OF LIFE

What This Chapter Will Do for You

Fear is engendered by a lack of understanding. This is particularly true of subjects like the religion of Witchcraft, and of the occult sciences. This chapter will give you understanding that will:

- Eliminate any fear of the occult Astromantic science
- Allow you to establish and define your nature
- Allow you to make long-term changes in your nature to gain automatically the life you want

Energy from Beyond the Stars

In the velvet of a desert night thou canst see in the vault of heaven as many stars as there are grains of sand on the beach of the Arabian Sea. The almighty Source of all our life, the god whom some worship that is called the Sun, is merely a very small one of these stars in the edge of the wheel of our galaxy—which itself is but one among many.[1] *During the 7,000 years when the Babylonians meditated on the differences between men born at various times of the year, they used the stars which were rising in the east at dawn as their calendar. They based their calculations on what my fathers told me was 370,000 years of observations; yet even these epochs are minute compared to the life of the great cosmos wherein we dwell. The constellations of stars that the Babylonians used were only the fingers of the clock, for it is the seasons of the year and the energies from beyond space which shape men to their natures, not which small local star appeareth at dawn. Yet we still use the names the Babylonians gave the seasons of the year, even though these constellations have moved on in their timeless progression. When thou viewest the sky, thou wilt look in vain for Regulus, the central star of Leo, on the horizon on 22 July. It dwelleth there no longer. Instead thou wilt see Castor and Pollux, the twins of Gemini.*

Thou Too Must See the Dawn

Each morning the daily rotation of the earth bringeth into view the almighty life-giving Sun. In their egotistical way, westerners say that the Sun 'rises;' yet in sooth all people know that it is our poor planet earth whose eastern bound doth sink from view so that we may view the immovable and eternal giver of life. If thou art to gain even the most minute understanding of the part thou playest and of thy

[1]We have given an illustration of this in Figure III-1——Gavin and Yvonne.

relationship to the great heavenly wheel, it behooveth thee to view the dawn as often as thou canst; for in this way, in the awe thou wilt feel for creation's boundless rhythmic pulsation, and in the power thou wilt gain therefrom, thy problems will be swept away and thou wilt be revitalized in the knowledge that thou art a part of this endless and wonderful drama. The ever-shining Sun giveth life, vitality, and energies to all beings carried into its shining rays by the rotation of their small planets. When thou hast viewed the dawn for several successive morns, thou wilt welcome those shining rays; and in welcoming them thou wilt be revitalized.

I do not think it necessary for thee to learn the arcane Arabic words with which my people welcome the Sun; but it is indeed wise for thee to acknowledge its presence, for in that way thou wilt realize more fully thou art a part of the great cosmos in which all live.

Greg Recharges Himself

Student File 4Y-3XA

Greg L works for a large aerospace concern in San Leandro. At the time he wrote to us he was having great difficulty in keeping up with his work; in the aerospace recession he feared he would be laid off because of the tremendous lassitude he could not seem to shake off. His problem basically stemmed from the fact that his job required that he travel between Los Angeles, Europe, and Australia at least once each month. He told us in his letters that when he first got the position, having won out over several rivals, he seemed to have plenty of vitality; but that recently this vitality had ebbed and had been replaced by a need to sleep continually. Before writing to us, he had visited no less than three physicians and a specialist; so he knew that there was nothing organically wrong and that his diet, if not perfect, was at least adequate.

First we asked Greg about any psychological problems

he might be having with his job or in his personal life; so far as we could tell from the replies, Greg was happily married with a wife who understood that when he was away for long periods he occasionally needed a woman's friendly companionship. Although he was worried because of the recession, he felt that in his area of the business, especially with the prospect of future sales in the Mideast, he should be secure—and, when he wasn't feeling sleepy, he was indeed most enthusiastic about his future prospects.

This puzzling case was resolved only through meditation. We found that though Greg had traveled around and walked outdoors in the foreign cities he visited when he was new to his job, he gradually had ceased this practice, especially when he found his first European lady friend. He began to stay more and more indoors; even when he came home, his attentive wife's having done most of the garden chores meant that he could stay indoors and enjoy her company more.

Greg simply was not receiving enough of the sun's vital energy. Coupled with the jet lag that repeatedly troubled him in his travel from one time zone to another, this put his whole system out of tune with the great natural circadian rhythm. (The circadian rhythm is the biological clock by which your body normally regulates itself; the regular changes from light to dark that allow you to know what time of day it is even without a watch.)

If you have to stay indoors a lot and travel frequently as Greg did, you lose the ability to know the time in your locale and even what season of the year it is. This means that your mind does not know when it is time to sleep and when it is time to eat, and the whole metabolism becomes confused and goes into a lethargic state.

Our meditation told us that this was Greg's specific problem. Additionally, our meditation indicated that he had recently come under great pressure in a fierce competition with a French firm for aircraft sales to Iraq. Our next letter to Greg gave him something of a shock: No one was supposed to know of the Iraqui negotiations, especially not a couple of Witches in Missouri! It was probably because of the jolt he got from this knowledge that he so closely followed our instructions. They were: "For the next month, never miss a sunrise."

That view of the sunrise totally changed Greg. From the lethargic, pallid salesman, he became once again a dynamic junior executive. With the rearrangements caused by the aerospace recession, and because his firm was not feeling the pinch as badly as others were—principally owing to Greg's sales efforts—he was promoted to sales manager. No longer needing to travel so often, he was able to spend more time with his wife and family in his own garden, naturally getting health-giving energy from the sun.

Your Personal Ritual of the Sunrise

If your body looks pallid and feels weary as so many do nowadays, you can immensely improve your looks and feelings by welcoming the sun each morning. Seeing the sun rise on its appointed track each day for as short a time as one month will completely change your nature. The steps in the ritual given below have been used since time immemorial; they are not difficult to follow.

Find for yourself a small, quiet place from which you can view the eastern horizon. Even in the midst of a city there will be a rooftop or some other place that you can use. From Table III-1 you can arrange your time so that you arrive perhaps thirty minutes before the rim of the sun appears above the eastern horizon. Sit comfortably and wait. Gaze intently at the horizon, and in this time consider your small problems. Turn your eye inward and examine your nature. Ask for guidance in your life. Suddenly as the sun appears you will see a light breaking through the darkness; for just as the sun illuminates the world, so your problems will be illuminated and answers will suggest themselves. As you watch the sun in its rapid climb into the heavens, with your mind contrast your problems with the sun's mighty power, its endless round when it illuminates millions upon millions of lives. Your problems will then appear far less dreadful.

As the sun clears the horizon, no matter what the weather, lay aside your robe and stand, so that the sun's vital life-giving energies can fall on your skin. You will find it beneficial to hold the palms of your hands toward the sun and to tilt your head back just a little. If you are standing on the natural earth, it is well to have your feet bare and to spread them perhaps 2½ feet apart. Stand thus for at least a minute, feeling the energy on your skin. Then put your robe on and begin your day refreshed, with more understanding of the real problems in your life and their relationship to the grandeur of the cosmos.

You have seen the great stars hanging in the firmament, and you can now understand that the energies received on our planet come from the furthest reaches of space. The energies that shape our being are not dependent on the small movements over a few hundred years of local stars; they are above and beyond that.

Do not return to bed after this observance of the sunrise; for if you sleep before beginning work, you will lose much of what has been gained.

Some people like to recite words of praise and thanks. In our opinion, words are so unworthy that we prefer simply to let our thoughts (which are also heard) speak for us.

1 Jan	7:15	1 July	4:10
15 Jan	7:10	15 July	4:20
1 Feb	7:00	1 Aug	4:35
15 Feb	6:40	15 Aug	4:50
1 Mar	6:20	1 Sept	5:05
15 Mar	6:00	15 Sept	5:25
1 April	5:30	1 Oct	5:35
15 April	5:00	15 Oct	5:55
1 May	4:40	1 Nov	6:15
15 May	4:20	15 Nov	6:35
1 Jun	4:10	1 Dec	6:55
15 Jun	4:05	15 Dec	7:10

Table III-1
Table of Dawn Times[2]

[2]When the Government plays games with the clocks in the months of summer, add one hour to the times above. In the United States, this converts Standard Time to Daylight Saving Time; example: on 1 June 4:10 becomes 5:10.

The Wheel Ever Onward Goes

Dost thou set out upon a journey without a map? Or without some guide as to where thou goest? The most important journey thou dost take is that through life's byways and alleyways. From what I have thus far taught thee, thou canst see how thy nature directeth thy footsteps. The changeless energies from beyond our poor universe bombard our small planet every hour of every day. As thou dost rotate under these changeless energies, each day can be likened unto a year of thy life. Thus in time that even I cannot remember, people learned to construct maps of life. They based these maps on the simple fact that as the earth rotates within the wheel of the universe, thou dost experience a microcosm of the next year of thy life so that a day becometh a year and several years of thy life merely a few days. Thus it was ordained billions of years ago when the universe was formed; and thus it will be when thy bones are but dust.

Julie Junior Was Not Hexed

Student File 2G-8PD

Julie C, a New York mother of five, named her youngest daughter after herself so that the girl became, of all things, Julie Junior. The mother had a tremendous interest in the occult and almost an obsession with astrology. Knowing that Julie Junior would be her last child, she shopped from astrologer to astrologer having chart after chart drawn, though she refused to acknowledge any 'negative' predictions. She maintained a perennial hope that something really extravagant would show up to make a special case of this little girl. Every astrologer who drew a natal chart for Julie Junior seemed to shake his or her head sadly over the terrible aspects that it showed. Julie Senior literally worried herself sick with her efforts to keep these bad aspects from affecting Julie Junior. As Julie Junior grew up, she could not help noticing her mother's concern and the peculiar way in which every so often she was kept in the house for several days. Julie Senior convinced herself that she was able to control the bad aspects of Julie Junior's chart and that the child was saved from a series of disasters only by her careful, diligent concern. Julie Junior was a bright child, and finally she asked her mother point blank what was going on. Instead of telling the truth, Julie Senior told her she was hexed, and that unless she followed the strict routine her mother asked of her, terrible things of the 'bogeyman will get you' variety would happen to her. The mother's attitude of unspecified dread badly frightened Julie Junior, and gradually she became introspective and withdrawn from the world. Her father Paige noticed these changes in his daughter, but Julie Senior was such a domineering woman that there was little he could do to soften Julie Junior's belief in the hex about which her mother constantly talked. The little girl went through her entire childhood with this 'hex' hanging over her. It followed her through puberty and blighted her life because the mother used it to justify denying her the dates and the freedom that her schoolmates enjoyed.

Finally, inevitably, Julie Senior's worst fears were realized. Julie Junior fell sick of a non-specific disease which just wasted her away. A friend of ours, a very capable astrologer from Phoenix, Arizona, was the last of a long series of astrologers that Julie Senior now consulted.

When Julie Senior told him that the little girl had avoided all the negative events foretold for her, he knew that there was something badly awry in the casting of her earlier charts; for although it is possible to avoid one or two negative aspects in a chart, no one can avoid them all for year after year. He questioned Julie Senior closely about the child's actual birth. He learned (not really to his surprise) that she had had a long difficult pregnancy with Julie Junior and that the doctors had finally induced labor. Thus the girl's birthdate was purely arbitrary and her birth time totally meaningless. The true birth time, the time at which Julie Junior should have been born under her correct influences, was quite different from the time at which she had been artifically forced into the world. Our astrologer friend then took significant facts from Julie Junior's life and constructed a horoscope that would fit those facts. This horoscope was far more positive than any of the previous ones which had been cast for her. It also showed clearly the onset of her present illness, but revealed that the illness would very rapidly go into remission.

Julie Senior was wiped out by the astrologer's revelations. She thought (rather selfishly) of all the work she had done to avoid the negative aspects which she had believed would affect Julie Junior. After she had overcome her shock, she began to think of how to tell her daughter that the 'hex' had been lifted. With Paige's prodding, she eventually told the truth; and after regaining her health, Julie Junior gradually began to lose her fear of the hex. The disillusion Julie Senior felt was so thorough that she no longer places so much reliance on natal charts as she used to; consequently she is not the astrology bore that she was, and those around her are far more comfortable in her presence. In fact she has gained many new friends.

The Microcosm and the Macrocosm

Figure III-1 shows more clearly than words can how the cosmic energies come from outer space and reach the earth. The circular band of astrological symbols represents the ancient timeclock that tells you which month of the year you are in. Thus once a year the earth is bombarded by each of the energies. This is what is called the macrocosmic effect. But—and this is a most important 'but'—during each day in the microcosm of our earth as it rotates on its own axis, you are also exposed to each of the energies. This is the microcosmic effect.

A day can therefore be equated to a year. This is how astrologers cast charts: They equate each day to a future year in your life. This is called 'progressing' a chart. Now the hour of your birth becomes important; for as the earth rotates, every two hours you come under the influence of a different energy. This is why errors in the timing of charts can so dramatically affect predictions or in fact a whole segment of life, as in the case of Julie Junior.

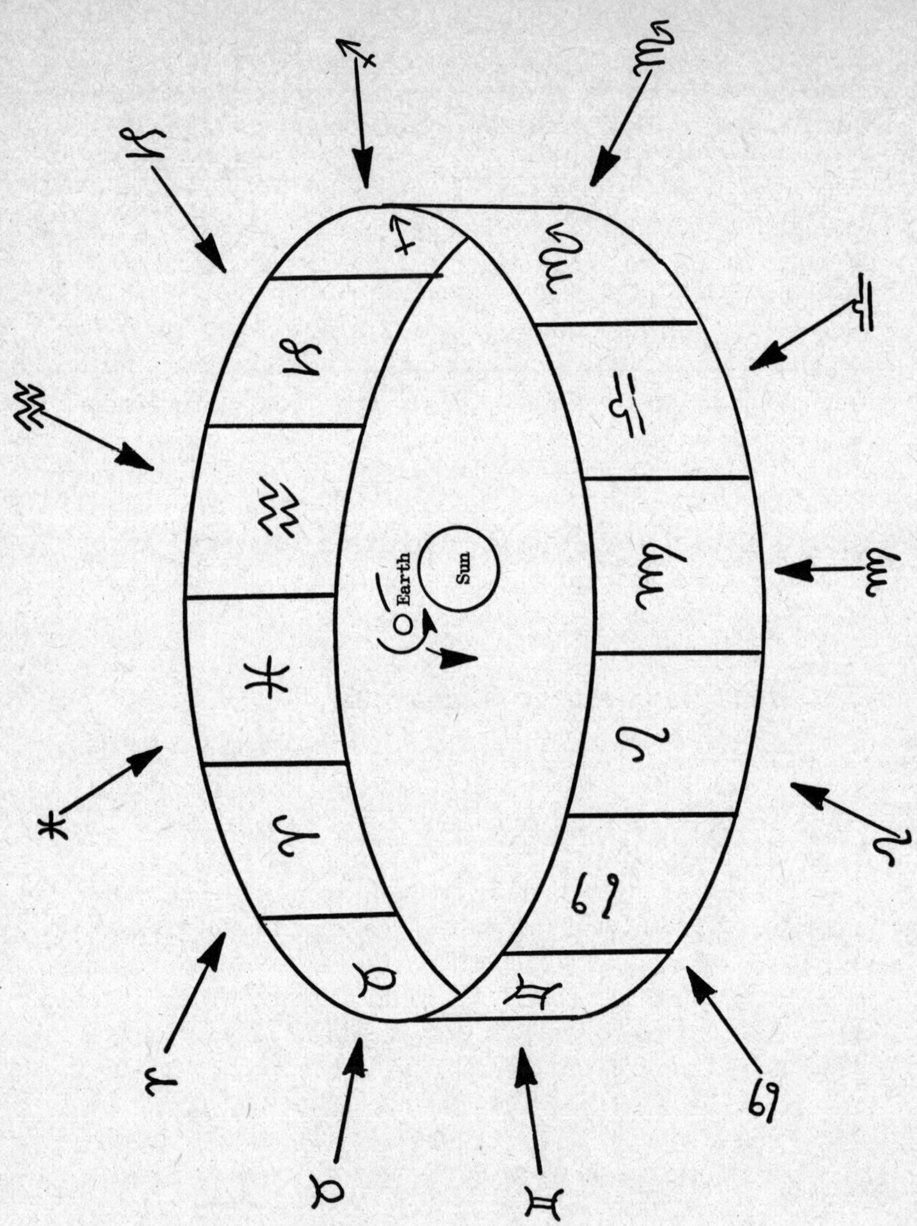

Figure III-1
The Energies from Beyond Space

Your 'sun sign' is the sign that was coming into view on the eastern horizon at dawn on the day of your birth.

Time Out in Thy Life

When the warrior is knocked senseless on the battlefield and is brought back from the grave by ministrations of the physicians, he oftentimes awakeneth as a different person. Sometimes a man is taken with a seizure, and when it passeth he too is changed. Study of such people by the learned men of old hath clearly shown that this time out of their lives doth affect their nature in important ways; that in fact they have been reborn into a new life and time. Sometimes in sooth it is to their benefit—but other times it is to their detriment. Even in thy life thou must have heard cases of such men as the successful merchant who had a seizure of the heart and became unable to deal with his associates in the harsh market in the competitive manner that made him successful.

Thou canst use this well-guarded secret to change thy life; for all thou hast to do is artificially pause in thy daily rounds and be reborn with the energies thou needest in order to be successful in thine endeavors. Just as the bear hibernates in winter, so thou canst take time out of thy life and become of a different nature.

Nothing in This World Is Changeless

No matter how thou complainest about thy life, at this moment thy life fitteth thee. It is the best life thy nature can obtain. Even though thou mayest feel thou art fitted for better things, still the world is a wonderful place in which to live and thou shouldst enjoy it as thou findest it. Though perhaps it liketh thee not, be assured that nothing is changeless. Even as the trees drop their leaves in winter, so thou canst change thy coloration and thy nature, and thereby change thy life. The trees drop their leaves and change their colors slowly, and thou must do the same. Decide on thy goal and change thy nature so that obtaining the objective is assured.

There are many mirages in the desert, and we all know that these mirages reflect real places; however, if thou hast no camel, thou canst never hope to reach the oasis of the mirage. First thou must acquire thy camel—and in this simile I mean the camel to represent the nature thou needest to gain thy desire. If thou art of a Magpie nature, it is exceeding difficult to become a merchant. If thou art of a Swan nature it is exceeding difficult to be faithful to thy spouse. Thus it is that thy nature must be changed as a first step on the short path to thine ultimate success. But be assured that thou canst change thy nature, merely by pausing a while in thy present state and awakening in the hour when the earth hath brought thee under the place in the heavenly firmament from which come the energies thou needest.

Mona's Death Revitalizes Her Life

Student File 2G-7NF

Mona P is now a highly successful advertising executive, though friends tell us that for many years she was a mousy nonentity. The change in Mona's life took place when she had what is now called the 'near-death' or 'return from beyond' experience. She was involved in a near-fatal car accident; and when she regained consciousness in a hospital after being 'out' for almost two days, she recounted the typical death-and-return encounter with Shining Ones (Beings of Light) that is now recognized as a genuine phenomenon undergone by many people.

From the mousy little woman that she had been, Mona returned a dynamic go-getting women's-libber. It was almost as if she had been possessed of a new spirit during the time she was unconscious. Her husband, who later divorced her, contacted us because he wanted an exorcism done so that his wife would return to her old doormat way of behaving; in the old way she never argued with him but always fell in immediately with his plans and suggestions. After we had analyzed her personality, we told him we could find no sign of a possessing entity and that we would therefore not even consider conducting an exorcism. We carefully reviewed the time of the accident, Mona's birthdate, and the time at which she returned to this world from her coma. We learned that the quiet Fish had in fact become a dynamic Scorpion. Mona was no longer satisfied, of course, with her housewifely role and quickly found herself a job with an advertising agency. That job allowed full range of her Scorpio cunning and determination.

Since that time she has never looked back; and recently she told us she was now earning in the five-figure bracket, but was planning to retire because she yearned for a quieter life. We took this as a clear sign that the change in her nature accomplished by the accident was wearing off.

Re-Enter the Womb and Be Reborn

The point is that you too can artificially do what was forced on Mona and on many other people. In Chapter I you learned how to perform a short-term reordering of your life. We will now give you a technique that will change you for many months; and sometimes, as in Mona's case, even for a year or two.

In order to take time out of your life artificially, you must go through a rebirth experience. This is accomplished by retiring from the world for a short period. Ibn Saud recommended that it be done by being buried alive; but we have found that if you confine yourself to a small, completely darkened room for the required period, the same effect is achieved as if you had actually been buried alive. An under-stair closet or something of that nature is quite large enough for this reordering of your life. We have even known people who achieved the result by curtaining off their bed and lying under it.

The best results are achieved when you sew or arrange to have sewn a tunnel of fabric through which you can crawl into and out of the small warm dark space you select for this experience. All you have to do is select a time when you will not be disturbed; go into your artificial womb under your own sign; and emerge from it under the sign that you desire to become.

Your Modern Guide to Changing Your Birth Date and Time

Thou must be forewarned that whate'er thou dost, it must be with a plan. I have cautioned thee before that thou needest a map for any journey and especially dost thou need a map for thy life. Using the techniques I taught thee, thou canst prepare a map showing how thou shouldst add energies to thy life. From this, thou canst decide what new sun sign will benefit thee most greatly. It is assuredly true that all the parts of thy life are interconnected and when thou changest one area of it thou inevitably changest the other areas as well. Thou canst not change thy nature without changing thine entire life, the relationships with thy friends, and with thy spouse and children. When thou deliberately redrawest the map of thy life, thou reconstructest the whole map, not part of it; for when the Wheel of the Heavens turneth above thy head, all its spokes turn as one. One spoke cannot turn without the others. Care and planning must therefore be observed so that thou gainest what it is that thou desirest, instead of some awful surprise for all thy work and planning.

Change Your Life This Month—Not Next

By following the steps outlined below, you can change your life.

1. *Choosing Your New Life*—First complete the work of Chapter II; then you will know which new sign will bring you the nature you need for success. Now look at Figure III-2. Trace out the two halves of the figure onto card, and pin them together at their centers. This 'Dial an Energy Unit' is de-

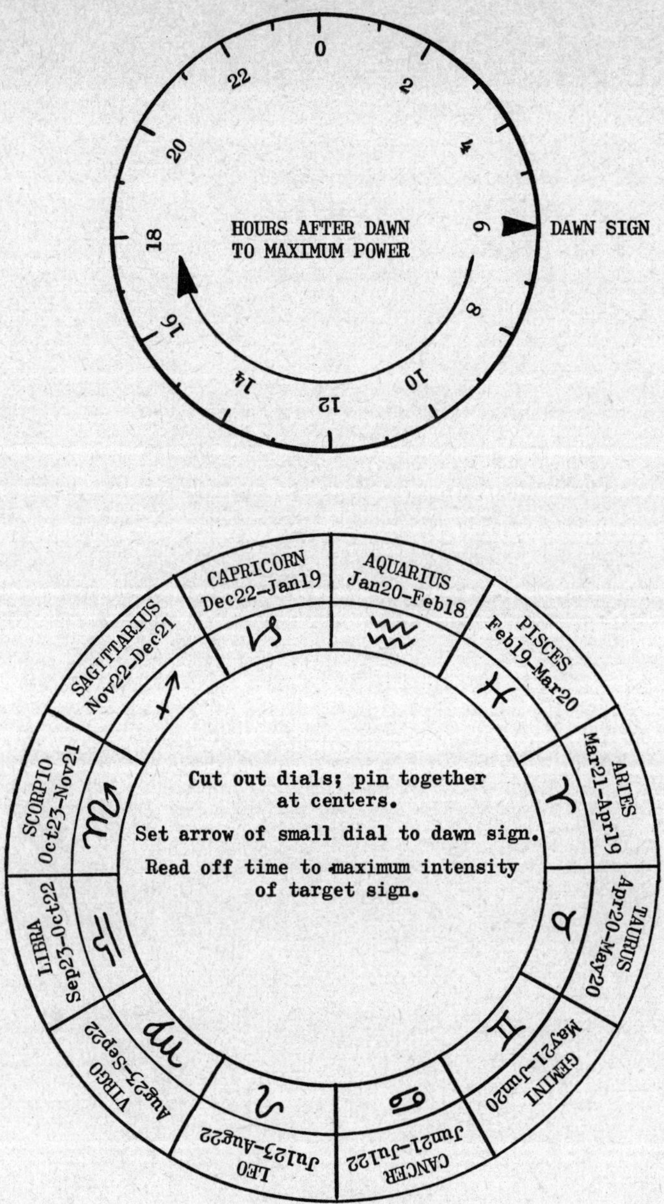

Figure III-2
Your Rebirth and Energy Power Dial

signed so that you can readily calculate the time between any two of the energies coming from different areas of the cosmos. You can also calculate the time after dawn that any desired energy will be available. See how many hours separate your present birth month from the one you want to have. Simply place the arrow on your present birth sign, and read off how many hours later the sign you want occurs. Figure III-3 shows a typical example, in which the subject goes from a Libra (Swan) to an Aries (Ram); that is, twelve hours. The dial is set for 1 June, when the dawn sign is Gemini.

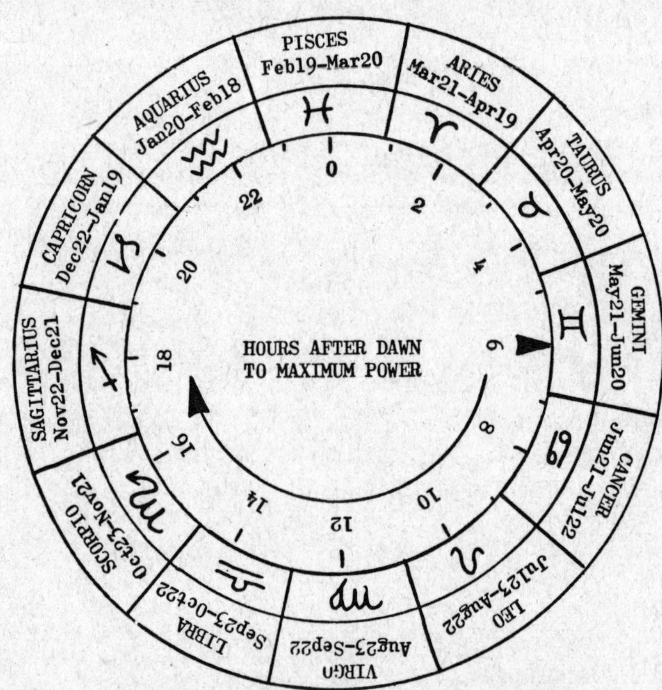

Example shows dial set for 1 June (Gemini). Subject wishes to change from Libra to Aries; enters womb 14 hours after dawn, and emerges 2 hours after dawn the following day.

Figure III-3
Example of Using Your Energy and Power Dial

2. *Necessary Equipment*—If the number of hours you calculate in Step 1 is small, all you will need is your warm room and something to lie on. If the time of transition is longer, however, you will need some simple food and water, and a container for body wastes. In either case, you will need a timer that you will be able to set and leave running outside your room so that from inside the room you can hear it go off. You are not allowed candles or reading material or radios or any distraction whatsoever in the room. The time you spend in being reborn is a time entirely apart from your life.

3. *Calculating the Time to Enter and Leave the Womb*—The new moon represents a time of new beginnings, and it is well to arrange your rebirth so that it occurs on a day soon after new moon. Look at your dial and set it for the dawn time of the day you have chosen. You can learn the time of dawn from your own observation of sunrise or from Table III-1. Then you will be able to see when during the day the two-hour period occurs that is the sign of your actual birth; that is, the sign you wish to forsake. You should enter your artificial womb at the center of this time period, and should set the timer so that you will leave your artificial womb at the center of the time period for the sign you desire to become. It is best to make sure that no one else will be in the area while you are undertaking your rebirth; for as we have said, this is a time apart, a time when you do not wish to be concerned with things of this world.

4. *Doing It*—Crawl into your artificial womb at the appointed hour and curl up on your bed in a position as close to the fetal position as you can manage; that is, knees under chin and arms wrapped around your folded legs. Whatever you do, be comfortable; for you will want to remain in this position for as long as you can. Lie there in the dark comfort of the artificial womb and think carefully of the new life you are about to enter. Imagine it in detail. Go over it again and again in your mind. Live each facet of it. See how it will be improved over your former life. Return to your childhood and imagine in your mind how events that went wrong in those early days

would have been more positive. Gloat a little, if you will, over the comfortable new life you are soon going to have. Doze and drift. Soon you will hear the timer. Now you must kick your feet out and make swimming motions with your hands. Stretch and take on your new identity. Crawl out through your tunnel into the world. Breathe as deeply as you can for a moment or two. If you feel like weeping, weep.

Many students say that they look on the world with new eyes after being reborn in this way; that clothes which they had previously thought perfectly satisfactory are no longer acceptable, so the first thing they have to do is go out and buy new outfits harmonious with their new color taste and personality.

Hal Modifies His Nature and Gains His Life's Ambition

Student File 4Y-5TR

A simple case to illustrate this method is that of Hal T, who wrote to us from Madison, Wisconsin. All his young life he had wanted to be a successful big-league umpire. He had undergone the necessary training and had scored some successes as a minor-league umpire. At that time we were at the height of our investigation into Ibn Saud's method, and we felt we had in Hal an ideal subject. He had been born with the nature of a Libra, and we suggested that to become a successful umpire he should attempt to change that nature to the more aggressive domineering Arian type. He carried out our instructions to the letter. It was obvious from his very next letter that dear, lovable Hal was now starting to become aggressive. Soon he got his heart's desire and became a major-league umpire.

"Welcome, Infant Soul"

When thou wast born into the world, thou wast allowed to take up thy tasks slowly. Thou didst go to school. Thou didst learn to sow and to reap under thy father's gentle tutelage. When thou art reborn and takest on a new identity, thou must learn to use that new identity slowly and carefully; otherwise thou wilt overreach thy capabilities. Just as the child learns, so must thou learn. The child takes many years to learn; but again, because of the correspondence between the heavenly wheel and the rotation of the planet on which thou livest, years can be replaced with days. Therefore thou shouldst spend as many days as thou art years old in learning to use thy new identity; for if thou dost try to hasten the process thou wilt surely slip back into thine old ways and habits, and all will have been in vain.

Chapter Four

ASTROMANTIC ASTRAL TRAVEL

What This Chapter Can Do for You

Who requires no disguise? Who cannot be seen? It could be you. You can learn to travel without your body, and by doing so, can spy on anyone you wish without his even having the least hint that you have 'overlooked' his life. Not only can you see what goes on, but you can also hear what other people are saying about you. Further, as you will see in this chapter, you can travel backward and forward in time. You can travel into the inner and outer realms of the spirit world where you can contact both your overself and higher intelligences to get many of your problems answered. Thousands upon thousands of people have learned how to accomplish this technique for traveling without the body. However, for most people it is a very hit-or-miss experience. Sometimes it works easily; sometimes great difficulty is experienced in their attempts to leave the body. In a previous book[1] we explained how these techniques could be used. Ibn Saud was rather critical of what we had told people to do, because he thought that (at least for some people) there is an easier method. After experimenting with his method, we have concluded that, as usual, he is absolutely correct.

As you progress through this chapter you will see how Astromancy plays a key role in the method Ibn Saud proposed. His method has now been tested with many hundreds of our School's students.

Esther Comes to Love Her New Neighbors

Student File 5G-4MA

Esther M is a widowed grandmother living alone in an apartment house in the Bronx, New York. She has been mugged several times and as a result of these muggings she took our course in Witchcraft to learn how to avoid any further repetition of these miserable experiences. Things were going quite well for Esther until her good friend and next-door neighbor, Golda K, and her husband moved to Florida. Their empty apartment was taken over by two leather-jacketed youngsters who to Esther were the epitome of all she feared. The man wore a black vest over old shirts with their sleeves removed; the girl favored black boots with painfully high heels, and the jeans she wore were even more greasy than her hair. Even the deadbolt and the chain on her door were not sufficient protection in Esther's mind from the evil and horror that the youngsters and their constant stream of visitors represented to her. Night after night she lay awake wondering

---

[1]"Magic Power of Witchcraft" G & Y Frost, Parker Publishing.

whether she would soon hear her door being broken down as a prelude to the rape and violation of herself and her beloved possessions that she dreaded. As she watched through the peep-hole in her door, she saw many small animals being carried into the apartment . . . yet very rarely saw any animals come out, and only very occasionally heard any animal-type sounds.

We told Esther to call the building superintendent or the police and report what she had seen. She did; but because in the past she had come to be known as a busybody and someone prone to cry 'Wolf!', they put her down as a paranoid meddler. Very little follow-up was done, for the police certainly couldn't get a search warrant on what little evidence Esther could provide them.

We ourselves astral-traveled to the apartment of Esther's new neighbors. We got a happy surprise when we found that they were actually caring for very sick animals and that they were the nicest of young people, people whom any neighbor would really like to know. Because of this happy surprise, we told Esther what was going on and that she should not worry; but just telling her was not enough. After several letters had passed back and forth in which Esther expressed more and more concern, we suggested that she try astral traveling with Ibn Saud's method; for we knew she had tried astral traveling before but had been unsuccessful.

Here then we had a very uptight lady, a subject whom most teachers of astral travel would have rejected as being far too tense ever to leave her body behind; however, in just three weeks Esther reported she had been able to travel to her neighbors' apartment. When she saw what they were doing, she offered to look after the animals while the young people went to their jobs each day. This was a tremendous relief to the young couple because they had often had to take days off to look after animals that needed constant attention. It has also been a boon to Esther, because now she has many friends in the younger community and realizes she had not only misjudged them but needed them as they needed her.

Anyone Can Astral Travel

If Esther can do it, you can do it. All it requires is the correct frame of mind which will allow you to leave your relaxed body behind while your spirit travels by itself. This is a perfectly safe and well-known procedure. You probably already astral travel every night when you dream. You may even have had that well-known 'deja-vu' experience, where you know that you have never actually visited a place—yet you feel totally familiar with it and can even tell precisely what you will see around the next corner. What has happened to you is this: You *have* in fact actually visited the place which you are now visiting for the first time *in your body*. Many scientific experiments have been conducted which prove that astral travel can be produced on demand, and that people can remember what they see and do during such trips. Various intelligence agencies in Russia and the United States have demonstrated that highly classified documents can be examined by the astral traveler even though the documents are sealed in steel vaults where security guards are on duty 24 hours a day.

At this point you may be afraid that something will happen to your spirit or your body if you dissociate them from each other. You must know that there is a solid, life-long connection between the two halves of yourself; and provided you follow directions when you trip out, no possible harm can come to your body. As soon as the least thing goes wrong in the environment of your body, your spirit will instantaneously be drawn back into it. How many times have you seen a child trembling on the edge of a swimming pool? How many times have you seen that same child a few short hours later thoroughly enjoying splashing about or even swimming in that same pool? Fear of the unknown is a terrible thing. All we can tell you is this: Just as in swimming, millions of people have done it before you; they have thoroughly enjoyed the experience and the power the technique gives them. If you don't take that first plunge, you will never succeed. We know that taking it is difficult; but be assured it is completely safe so long as you follow a few simple directions.

Helping Yourself to Leave Your Body

Certain people by nature are far more relaxed than others. As thou knowest, this hath nothing to do with thine intelligence or aught else except the sign in whose time thou wert born. Thus it followeth naturally that if thou choosest the correct personality thou wilt be able to relax and leave thy body. Verily, for each endeavor thou canst possibly imagine, there is a time of birth appropriate; for as thy poor planet carries thee under the great Wheel of the Heavens, so thou dost enjoy all the benefits that these powers from beyond thy universe bestow on thee. In the land of the Pharaohs in time before time was born, surgeons discovered that if a body was detached from its spirit, serious operations could be undertaken without harm. People set at hard labor for their sins can tell thee that they also can leave their bodies and watch them tirelessly work. But this technique of detaching was lost, as many other great discoveries have been lost, when the Christian destroyer Gregory commanded that the great works of antiquity recorded in Egyptian papyri be destroyed.

The great secret of the travel of thy spirit without thy body was contained in the great library of Alexandria which the woman mathematician and librarian Hypatia did defend unto her death at the hands of the Christian. At great risk and sacrifice, small fragments of this knowledge were carried unto the Sheik Abdullah Al Mamun, who in our "City of Peace." Dar-al-Salam, translated and kept these sacred fragments so that knowledge would not be lost to the people of the Prophet. Inshallah! It is this great knowledge that I, Ibn Saud, will now reveal to thee.

Gunter Survives the Car Crash

Student File 4Y-3AW

Gunter V worked as an aerospace sales manager for a major concern in West Germany. He spent much time in the United States, culminating in a two-year assignment in southern California. While he was in southern California he learned to astral travel, and became acquainted with all the minor benefits of this skill. He found, for instance, that when he visited the dentist he could readily leave his body in the chair and from a spot near the ceiling could watch the dentist perform his work, feeling none of the pain or the fear that usually accompanied such visits.

Gunter little knew how soon his capability would be put to the test. The second day after his return to Germany, he set out to visit his father in the Bavarian mountains. He must have forgotten the difference between the no-speed-limit travel on German autobahns and the slow speed limit in the United States. He lost control of his car on the autobahn, and totaled it. He was trapped within the car; and although he was losing only a little blood, he was in terrible mind-blinding pain. He knew that if he didn't get out of his body he would soon die, for the pain was so intense that no one could have endured it for long and kept his sanity. Somehow even in this terrible situation he managed, as he had done so many times before, to leave his body. Immediately the pain disappeared. He could see his body grotesquely twisted in the shattered car, yet he could feel no pain. Soon he saw the ambulance coming and the autobahn police rescue squad working to release his body from the wreckage. He followed closely as his body was transported to the hospital. He watched intently as the doctors set the twisted limbs. He listened as they said, "Now it is in the hands of the gods. As soon as he recovers consciousness we will be able to tell whether he is going to make it."

Tentatively Gunter slipped back into his body. Yes, it was painful; but not unbearably so. He opened his eyes and stirred. From there on his recovery was rapid. Several times the hospital physicians told him what a good thing it was that he was unconscious when he was brought in; for if he had been conscious, they felt his mind might have been damaged by the pain. Of course Gunter never told them that his unconsciousness was intentional.

Your Basic Astromantic Astral Travel Technique

In the midst of his diatribe against the people who killed Hypatia, Ibn Saud gave us the clue to the secret of successful astral travel. You must change your personality so that you can relax and travel without your body. This brings us to the essential fact: It is the *spirit* that travels and goes on, and it is the *spirit* which is affected by the techniques which Ibn Saud recommends. In an ancient holy book, the Rig Veda, it is written that your spirit and your body are like a driver and a chariot; and it is said that the reins of the chariot are Wisdom. The spirit drives and controls the chariot just as you drive and control an automobile. You would not drive an automobile that you couldn't make obey your commands. It is the real You, the spirit, that is in control; and you—the real You—who is affected by Astromantic forces. It is not your body that you change; it is the spirit.

If you wished to compete in the Olympic Games, you would have to train your body so that it was like a fine-tuned racing car. That might not be possible, though; your body may be in the shape of a good old comfortable family sedan. You cannot expect a sedan-style body to respond to a spiritual command that tells it to do something beyond its capability. However, you can and should expect that the spirit remain in control and can direct the body to do almost everything that is needed to make your life easy and comfortable. This is especially true with respect to astral travel.

The personality of your spirit may be such that you are too tense to leave your position of control behind the steering wheel, like the people who drive into a hamburger stand and instead of eating comfortably at a table, eat their hamburger on their lap in the car. Remember: The spirit is in control. It can leave the body any time it wishes, without risk.

Experimental results clearly show that those people who are born in the time of Cancer the Crab have the personality which most easily allows their spirit to travel astrally. Thus you should modify your personality to that of a Cancer, using the technique we have previously shown you, before you start the experimental procedures that will allow you to leave your body. We suggest that you do not use a rebirth system for this, but rather the very simple technique described in Chapter I. Once you have satisfactorily modified your personality to that of a Cancer, you should proceed as follows:

1. *Equipment*
   - A. Find a comfortable chair. It should be constructed of wood or of wood and fabric; there is to be in its makeup no iron or steel and an absolute minimum of non-ferrous metal. Further, it should contain no materials of animal origin, such as wool, leather, bone, or silk.
   - B. Find a quiet-running timer.
   - C. Find a loose robe of cotton.
   - D. Find a container of salt.

2. *Location*—Select a place. Somewhere in your home there is a spot suitable for your work. The requirements are, in order of importance:
   - A. A solid wall running north and south.
   - B. An area along that wall that is not near heavy electric cabling or metal objects.
   - C. An absolute minimum of clutter. Books and newspapers are particularly undesirable because of the busy thought patterns they engender.
   - D. A location as close to the sky as possible.

3. *Time*—Establish a time for this practice, and stick with it. The factors influencing the hour chosen vary from

individual to individual, but here are some things that should be considered.

A. When will you be able to be uninterrupted?

B. Can you keep this appointment every day unless something unforeseen interferes?

C. Will your mind be free of petty work and household problems during the selected time?

D. Is the sun below the horizon at the time you have chosen?

4. *Getting Things Arranged*—If your wall is not quite true north-south, arrange the chair so that you face the cardinal point. Subdue the light entering the room. Turn off any mechanical contrivances; shut off the power from nearby cables. Use the salt to draw an unbroken circle around you clockwise on the floor. Sit in the chair you have selected with your back to the wall, preferably facing eastward (though westward is also acceptable). Set the timer for fifteen minutes. Have your legs uncrossed, your hands resting with palms up on your thighs. Tilt your head back very slightly. Absolutely relax all muscles in your body. Open your aura, the protective force field around you. Lay back your robe at the front while you mentally picture yourself surrounded by a pale white glow or halo of light. When you are settled and comfortable, with your eyes closed say aloud, "Spirits of mischievous intent, spirits of lower entities, you cannot cross this sacred line." As you say this affirmation, imagine yourself sitting at the center of a sphere of blue-white light. You are surrounded above and below by a complete, impenetrable sphere of protection.

5. *Getting Out*—Visualize yourself standing outside the salt circle looking back at your relaxed body. Imagine yourself outside the circle. Visualize as clearly as you can what your body looks like sitting in the chair. Now step a pace backward and see how the vision changes. When you can clearly visualize yourself from these two positions, move your vantage point up and away to a corner of the room so that you

are now looking down at your recumbent body. Visualize this scene for a few minutes. Now return to your body. Then repeat this stepping-out and returning procedure.

6. *Traveling*—When you are comfortable with leaving your body and returning to it, begin to imagine the place where you wish to be in the space-time continuum on your first long astral trip. Will yourself to see the scene in great detail in full color, and hear the people speaking. Suddenly, click! Just like learning to ride a bicycle, you will actually be there. The realization that you are actually some place else sometimes makes you abruptly snap back into your body. If this happens, as you have learned, start over again; follow the steps: First the step outside the circle, then the step backward, then to the corner of the room, then to the place you want to go. This time you will be able to do it more quickly, and the realization that you have actually left your body will not be such a surprise; consequently you will be able to stay longer in the astral travel mode.

Occasionally you may hear music or a buzzing noise as you go into the mode. Do not be afraid; these are common occurrences, though we cannot fully explain them yet. Soon your spirit will learn by itself to come back into the body just a few moments before the bell of your timer rings. The body knows that the timer is about to ring, and brings the spirit back so that it is not shocked. Fifteen minutes a day is quite enough for anyone to astral travel. Even though you will feel uplifted when you come back, still it is an escape from the real world: an escape in which it is easy to overindulge yourself.

When you come back and are ready to re-enter the mundane world, we recommend you make some simple statement as you imagine your aura or field closing about you. The following is popular:

> "I am surrounded by the pure white light of the God.
> Nothing but good shall come to me;
> Nothing but good shall go from me."

Now leave your circle. If you need to go away from your

residence any time within the next hour or so, we recommend a quick wash in cold water to bring you to earth.

For reasons that we are hard put to explain, even with the personality change explained in the previous section, some people still have trouble getting out of their body. Ibn Saud again gave us the clue as to what the problem was when he said 'personality and *time.*' In order to make getting out of your body an absolute certainty, we have found that you must make sure that the correct energies are impinging on you from outer space.

Friedrich Makes a Fortune in Deutschmarks

Student File 2Y-8ZW

Friedrich K lived in Ulm, West Germany. He was a very close friend of Gunter V, whom we discussed in the last example. Gunter taught Friedrich to astral travel; however, Friedrich could not always get out of his body. In his Teutonic way this greatly annoyed him, because he felt that if a thing worked it ought to work every time. Gunter first wrote to us explaining Friedrich's problem; then Friedrich himself enrolled in our School and sought our aid to advance his understanding to such a level that when he tried something in the psychic world it would work every time. After much frustration he learned (as many before him had) that psychic activity is not all that cut and dried. However, in working with Friedrich we did discover that the time element, which Ibn Saud had mentioned only in passing, was tremendously important in successful astral travel. We instructed Friedrich to attempt his astral travel only at the appropriate time; and he reported with elation that he could now astral travel almost every time he tried it.

As a test of his powers, without telling us, Friedrich took a tremendous gamble. He had a friend invest all his money in Deutschmark futures, and every day he astral traveled to the big banks in the United States and Germany to hear what the bank officials were saying about the next day's movement of the dollar: How far would the dollar drop? Remember: Every Deutschmark Friedrich had invested had a leverage of thousands of dollars. This meant that in one day he could lose hundreds of thousands of Deutschmarks, which would be more than his entire life savings. But through his ability to astral travel consistently, Friedrich was there the day before the United States put into operation its 'save the dollar' program. He was able to tell his broker to sell at opening on that fateful morning when the Deutschmark began its long slide against the dollar. That slide cost even many of the big banks who were not in the know millions of dollars and Deutschmarks. When Friedrich sold, he was over $2,000,000 ahead of the market. He sold against all his broker's advice; but by mid-morning that day, the broker was congratulating him on his smart move. Friedrich confided to us, "It wasn't by any means a smart move, because I knew precisely what was going to happen."

Your Sure-Fire Ticket to Astral Travel

When you have acquired the right (Cancer) personality to fit your spirit temporarily for astral travel, you must time your sessions so that you are in your chair, in your protective circle, when the Cancerian energy is raining down from beyond the stars. Ascertain the time of dawn on the day you plan to travel. Then with your calculator dial from Figure III-2, compute the time when the Cancerian energies will be at their most powerful. Figure IV-1 shows the dial set for a typical January day when dawn occurred at 7:13. From it you can see that Cancer energy is at a maximum around 24.13 or 13 minutes after midnight (seventeen hours after dawn). This step makes that essential, critical difference. It will allow you to fulfill your dream and travel without your body to see what friends are doing and saying, and even to learn what tomorrow holds for you.

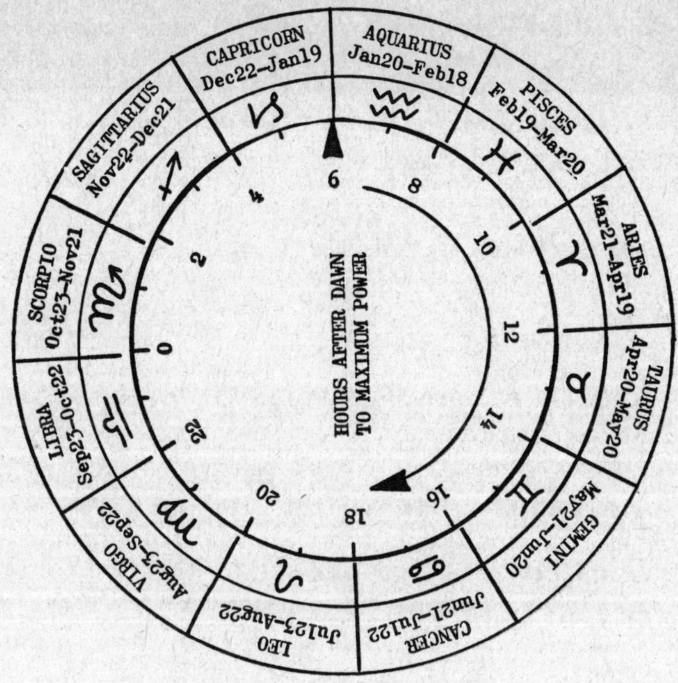

Dial set for January 19 (dawn at 7:13 a.m.)
Maximum energy occurs 17 hours after dawn.

Maximum Cancer	17	hours after dawn
+	7:13	
	24:13	or 13 minutes after midnight

Fivure IV-1
Your Astral Travel Guide Dial

Traveling to Realms Unknown

We have spoken of traveling to visit friends and of traveling forward and backward in time. These travels may be considered to be all on your own plane of existence, for you are not traveling into areas of the unknown. Even if you elect to go out and touch the moon or the sun astrally, still you are traveling in your own familiar field of reality; you are not exploring any unknown or uncharted region. In fact, once you have learned how to travel in these mundane realms, you can start to learn how to travel into other realities, realities which only barely touch our own.

Winona Releases Her Mother's Spirit

Student File 3G-1BG

Winona K was one of our students in St. Louis when we lived there. She came to us because her late mother was haunting her. Every time Winona relaxed, her mother would appear and order her around, tell her to do more with the children, or even direct her in what to make for dinner. The psychic link between Winona and her mother was a continuation of a very domineering relationship the mother had formed during Winona's childhood. Poor Winona got no rest. Everything she did, it seemed, her mother disapproved of. Her sex life too deteriorated, because she always had the uneasy feeling that Mother was watching her every move.

We taught Winona how to meditate, but that really helped very little—because all she got in meditation was Edna's domineering features and more instructions. We instructed Winona: Tell your mother firmly that she should leave and progress, because she is only holding up her own progress. Edna answered, with even more firmness than usual, that she couldn't possibly leave while Winona's life was in such a mess. It was obvious to the indignant mother that Winona was quite incapable of running a household, bringing up children, or even making love. Furthermore, Edna told her to stop seeing 'those Witches' who were interfering in her life and with the communication between mother and daughter, and get back to church. As a last and very firm point, in bolstering her refusal to leave, she told Winona that until an angel came for her she was going to stay where she knew she was welcome.

Something drastic had to be done. We took the easy way out. Gavin went into the astral plane and faked up a white nightie and a pair of big wings to wear to Winona's apartment. In this guise he led Edna out of the apartment and into a higher realm.

Consulting Ibn Saud's Friends for a Better Life

Once you start traveling into other realities, you will find that you can put on any guise you can think of. You can be the queen in her court; you can be the lord of the manor or the sultan in his harem. Further, you will find that language is no barrier, for all communication is in a telepathic style that requires no language. Thus if you wish, you can communicate with any spirit, even with Ibn Saud himself. If you have a question about this work or about any problem that may be troubling your life, you can visualize a Master who would naturally have the answer to such a question; then in astral travel you can ask the Master for the answer you need. Thus you can become knowledgeable in any subject that has ever been studied in this or other universes.

Chapter Five

HEALING AND REVITALIZING YOUR BODY AND LIFE WITH ASTROMANCY

What This Chapter Can Do for You

Reading this chapter may be the most important thing you ever do; for even if you and your loved ones are in the best of health, still you will find information in this chapter that will keep you young and will revitalize the rest of your life. Additionally it will teach you how to:

- Avoid the afflictions of age
- Reduce fevers
- Accelerate the healing of broken limbs
- Overcome nervousness
- Increase your sexual potency
- Give you inner youth

In Ibn Saud's day the law was extremely fierce with regard to medical malpractice. Doctors could be hanged or blinded, or have their hands cut off, for minor errors. With such severe penalties, only the best of physicians survived. Thus the knowledge that Ibn Saud has to pass on to us is both practical and proven.

Thy Body Is Thy Temple

If thou wert to set out on a journey across the Arabian desert, thou wouldst be sure to have a good riding camel on which to travel. Thy spirit is to thy body as the rider is to the camel. If thou ridest thy camel too hard and dost not care for it, thou runnest the risk of dying in the desert. Thus it furthereth thee to look after thy camel.

Thy body is the temple in which dwelleth thy spirit. It is given unto thy care by the great god, Allah akbar. When thou disregardest thy body, thy spirit doth suffer. As thou hast learnt, all spirits do have their own natures: natures which are dependent on their birthdate. Thus by their nature some spirits drive their bodies hard and others offend against Allah by failing properly to feed and maintain their bodies. I say unto thee that all natures have certain characteristics which tend to cause corresponding types of damage to the temple of the body.

The least pressure on the body, if it be continued for a sufficient passage of time, will damage it. The breeze from the seacoast doth blow on the rock-hard mountain; in time it doth carve the mountain into grotesque shapes. As it is with the rocks, so it is with thy body: Any continuous pressure doth make thy body bend to its will. It mattereth not whether that force cometh from thy birth nature or from pressures around thee in thy home or from the place where thou performest thy appointed task. If thou dost not keep a balance in thy life, thou wilt assuredly become ill. Thus too it is that when thou strivest mightily, always in one direction, for a new love or for wealth or for any good, thou dost for a short time assuredly unbalance thy life; and in these times too thou must guard thyself against the sickness that imbalance doth engender. When thou art ill, thou must bring the energy from the cosmos to help rebalance thy life and cure thine affliction.

It is assuredly true that if thy diet be poor thou wilt need to correct this; for thy body doth need good food just as the camel doth. But when thou are sorely afflicted, it is thy spirit that needeth to be cared for and balanced first. Thus it was, and thus it is, that thou canst use the energies from beyond space to cure and repair thy spirit so that thy body is at rest, in balance, and vitally healthy.

Dancing Cures the Children's Ills

Nicholas V is a retired ballet dancer and choreographer who lives in New York's inner city. Mostly because of his interest in ballet, Nicholas opened a small dance studio for local children. His very low fees and the natural instincts of both hispanic and black children for drama and dance guaranteed that his studio would be a success. Nicholas noticed on open nights, when parents were invited to come and see their children dance, that many of them brought other children who seemed interested but who would not participate. The parents told him these children would never dance, citing all sorts of quite insignificant illnesses and flaws. One child was said to have acne; another was described as too plump; yet another was introduced as 'too tall;' and so on, and so on. . . The list was as varied as were the children themselves.

One night in a dream, Nicholas saw himself taking all these children and making world-famous dancers of them. In his dream they all had perfect unblemished bodies and poise enough to appear before royalty. The dream was so vivid that the very next day Nicholas invited the parents of these children to discuss the possibility of forming an entire class from their ranks. He made no charge for this class, and the parents responded well to his offer. But the first meeting of the class was a near-disaster, for Nicholas simply could not get through to these young people, who had learned to regard themselves as handicapped. That evening he called us to discuss the difficulty. We meditated on it and called him back to suggest this: He should let the kids each pick one of the twelve ancient animal symbols of the heavens and invent a dance for that animal. We warned him that the kids should be allowed freely to select the animal and that their dance too should be entirely freestyle, without guidance. The children displayed a great deal of pleasure in doing this, and visibly opened up in their communication with Nicholas.

Under our direction, in the second session Nicholas selected the animals that the children were to dance instead of letting them choose their own. Again the children responded well; and though they danced with less assurance, still they danced. Over the next few weeks, a dramatic change occurred in the natures of those children. Their dancing became more lively. Magically the shyness, the weakness, the cringing posture, the minor blemishes vanished. For as the children danced, each was gathering from the cosmos the energy he needed to make himself whole.

Your Healing Wheel of the Cosmos

Over the past half-century or so, doctors have recognized with growing clarity the part played by the mind in illness and health. The pressures of modern society, the need in the west always to appear young and virile, the soul-destroying repetitive work of the machine age, have all combined to damage the spirit and increase to intolerable limits the stresses borne by body and spirit. No one can yet tell precisely how the relationship between disease, mind, and body works; yet since the pioneering work done by Sigmund Freud, many have demonstrated the dramatic changes that can be wrought in a person's health by probing and correcting problems in his mind. The stage hypnotist can raise a burn-blister by touching his subject with a pencil; equally, he can make that blister go away simply by saying, "I didn't burn you." He has effected a cure—a cure that is just as valid as any wrought by Jesus or by Katherine Kuhlmann or by any other healer, even though he did not call on God to help.

Because you were born at a specific time of year and thus

have a particular nature, you will run your body in a certain way; this will cause it to have certain characteristics and be susceptible to certain diseases, by its very nature. Someone who was born six months away from your birthdate, that is, on the opposite side of the Wheel, will have strengths and weaknesses complementary to yours. This is shown in Figure V-1, which is a cosmic wheel set out to show the diseases that are common to the various birthdate natures and the sign of the months whose energies will help those illnesses.

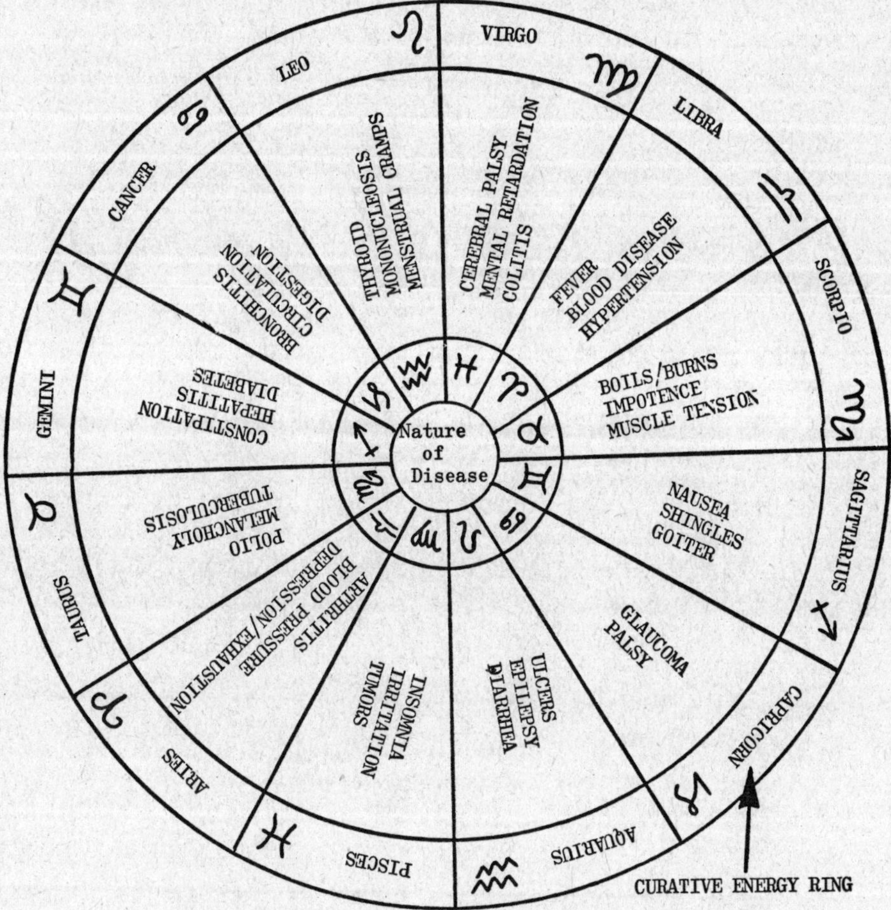

Look at inner ring for disease. Use energy of outer ring for cure.

Figure V-1
Your Heavenly Healing Wheel of the Cosmos

Let us take the case of Aries and Libra. These two months are precisely opposite each other on the wheel. Notice that Aries is a high-energy sign; someone suffering from depression or exhaustion or arthritis, for instance, can greatly benefit from Arian energy. Those diseases are most common to Libra-natured persons. The reverse is also true: Because the Aries nature is so high-energy, it tends to hypertension and fever, with associated diseases of the blood. The energy of the quiet, friendly Libra nature will cure these high-energy diseases. All you have to do, then, to help cure any illness is to locate it on your Cosmic Healing Wheel and see what energy is required to aid in the cure. All Nicholas did with the children was encourage them to dance the dance of the animal which is opposite the one they originally selected; for in this way he balanced their energy and cured the diseases of their natures.

To bring into your life or into the life of a friend the energy you lack, all you need to do is follow the recommendations we gave you in the very first chapter of this book. Even if you do not have symptoms of a particular illness, still if you bring into your life some of the energy from the sign opposite your own, you will feel refreshed and revitalized.

The Microcosm Reflects the Cosmos

Thy body is made up of many parts, and each part is made up of many elements. Similarly thy spirit hath many natures. It is the combination of these natures which together give thee thy unique personality. The cosmos above thee also hath many parts: stars and planets, asteroids, empty space; together all make up this and other universes. The energies that form the nature of thy spirit come from the heavens above thee. The heavens make a perfect balance; in them nothing is out of place. Thy spirit too must be balanced; and after thy spirit, thy body must be balanced. Thy body can be looked upon as a minute cosmos, a microcosm that is a reflection of the great cosmos in which thou dwellest. As thou gazest at the stars above, thou canst see the beauty and the symmetry of the handiwork of Allah; and it behooveth thee to be as balanced in thy body and in thy life as are the heavens above thee. If thou canst achieve a balanced spirit and a balanced body, success, vitality, and virility will assuredly be thine. Thus to achieve the balance thou needest in thy perfect body, thou must imitate the handiwork of Allah manifested in the heavens.

Thou wert born under one particular arrangement of the heavens. Thou reflectest only one segment most strongly. Thus thy nature is unbalanced, and unless thou correctest it, thou wilt be subject to the illnesses of thy nature. Thou canst not help what thou wast born to be. But harken to my words: Thou canst bring in the energies which thy nature lacketh; and by bringing in these missing energies, thou canst rebalance thy spirit and achieve perfection of both thy nature and thy body.

Lorrie Cures Walt's Crippling Gout

Student File 5G-6EC

Lorrie K is a student of the School from Monterey, California. She was widowed in her early thirties, but was left quite comfortably off at the death of Gardner, her businessman husband. She lived a quiet life, working occasionally as she grew bored by the normal round of clubs and charities with which she filled her life. We suspect she started taking our course purely to fill some empty hours. Through letters, we grew quite friendly with Lorrie; we shared her joy when, after more than ten years of widowhood, she met "Mr. Right" on the tennis courts of her local club. Even though Mr. Right was considerably older than she, still they were well matched, since Lorrie tended to be a homebody and Walt tended to be outgoing. Thus the discrepancy in their ages was overcome by the differences in their basic natures.

Everything seemed to Lorrie to be progressing well, when one day Walt called and abruptly broke off a tennis date they had made. That point marked a definite freezing of Lorrie out of Walt's life. As you can imagine, Lorrie—who was in love for the first time since Gardner's death—was extremely upset by this sudden change of attitude. She wrote to us to ask us whether we could do a love spell so that Walt would marry her. We told her quite forthrightly that she should first find out from Walt what the problem was. She should, if you like, face him down with it. This was not Lorrie's natural behavior, so we told her how to take on the aspects of a Capricorn and then to find out precisely what the problem was.

Lorrie transformed herself into a perfect example of the rather abrasive Capricorn mold. She drove to Walt's home and literally forced her way past his housekeeper into his study. A very emotional scene ensued. Lorrie kept control of her Capricorn self and did not weaken until Walt finally blurted out, "Damn it, Lorrie, I couldn't keep our date. I had gout!"

Lorrie was flabbergasted. "Gout! Why on earth couldn't you tell me?"

Walt confessed that as he saw it, gout was an old man's disease; it meant that he was too old to be squiring around a young and beautiful thing like Lorrie. He just knew that their relationship must go no further, because she was so much younger than he that he was bound to fall apart physically while she was still in the prime of her life.

Lorrie was smart enough to put away her Capricorn abrasiveness at this point and become her normal loving self. In this mode she told Walt that she didn't give a damn about the difference in their ages, that she had had one marriage that had lasted only five years until Gardner's death; that she was willing to risk another relationship for as few days, months, or years as the gods gave her; and that she would rather be with Walt for a year than alone for the rest of her life. "Anyway," she concluded, "I'm sure we can cure your gout." Between Astromantic power and a change in diet, she soon proved that Walt's gout was not the insurmountable problem he had believed it would be.

Like two young lovers, they decided they would try out their new relationship by living together for a time before committing themselves. The very night Lorrie moved in with

Walt it became obvious that he was still a virile lover. The next morning as she turned to him, he confessed, "I was afraid you would laugh at me." Her only reply was a drowsy smile.

The Parts of the Wheel and the Body of Man

The interconnection between the cosmos, the human body, and illness has been acknowledged and recorded for centuries. Figure V-2 shows the relationship in the Health Wheel of the Heavens. Notice how each part of the body is

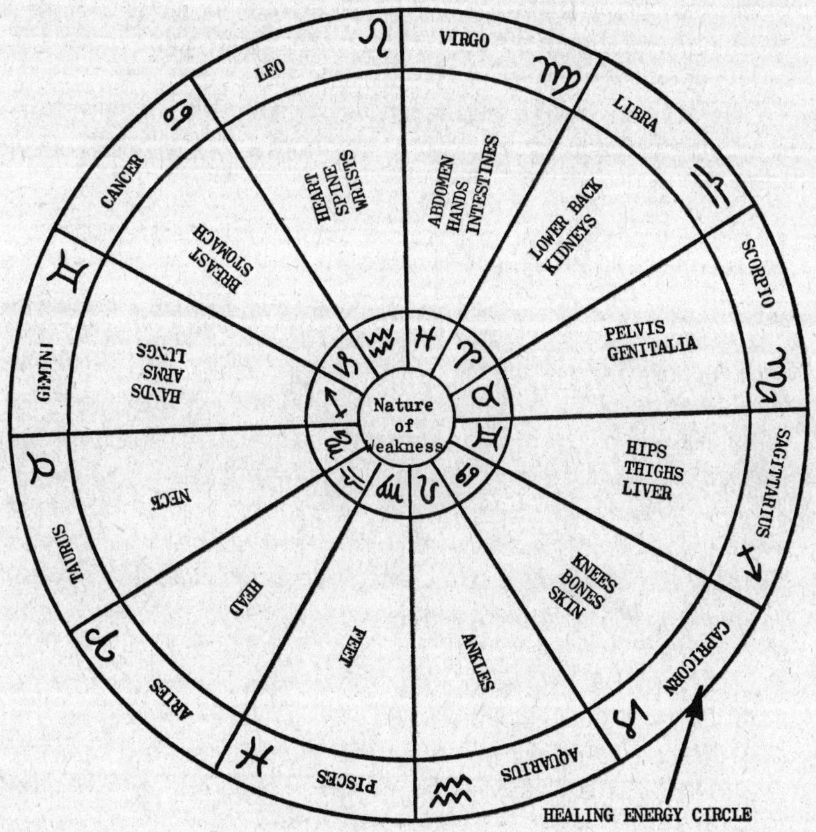

Figure V-2
Your Cosmic Health Wheel of Body Parts

opposite one of the natural birth months. Thus if you have weaknesses in any one of your body's parts, you can overcome it by adding energy of the correct month: energy to reinforce and strengthen the problem area. Since this is a matter of a temporary weakness, you need only to carry out the procedure outlined in Chapter I; there is no need to go through the whole rebirth procedure. If you look at Figure V-2, you can see that gout comes under the foot area; and in order to overcome problems in this area, energy from the month of Pisces must be applied. Lorrie applied that energy, together with some invigorating Arian energy. This gave Walt the extra vitality and thrust he needed on their first night together.

We do not know whether Walt's problems were caused by his fear of getting entangled with a younger woman or by a natural weakness in his feet. It didn't make any difference; the energies worked anyway.

Walt and Lorrie did marry, and until their move to Bermuda were frequent visitors in our home.

To Every Healing the Appropriate Hours

The great Watchers from the ziggurats noted that there was an hour appropriate to all things. They also observed that there was an hour appropriate to healing, but that this hour varied as our planet turned under the wheel of the heavens. Thus they observed that to cure the desert flux at one season of the year there was an appropriate hour, but that when this poor planet turned so that another season came in its due course, the hour for curing the flux did change. Years of study on these matters convinced the great mathematicians and astrologers of ancient time that energies from beyond the cosmos did aid in the cure of every disease and that in attempting a cure, a doctor should look with care to the state of the heavens so that he could direct the appropriate cosmic energies to his patient. It little profiteth thee to attempt a cure when the time is out of joint; for if thou dost, thou wilt surely fail. As the Christian Bible doth direct thee, there is a time for all things and a little patience will soon bring to thee the time for any healing; for in every revolution of the planet thou dost receive a fair portion of each of the healing energies.

It behooveth thee also every day of thy life to absorb some of these energies to replace the energy thou dost expend at thy appointed task. The rug-maker's back doth become weary and his hands stiff through the constant sameness of his task; the scribe's eyes become weak and watery. Each day at the appropriate hour, thou shouldst replace these energies and repair the damage thou dost to thy body.

Arthritic Annalie Leaves Her Wheelchair

Student File 6G-3HY

Annalie and Roger Q live in a mobile home in a park in Florida, where they retired at the very young age of 45 from a farm in Idaho. They both hoped to become writers; however, they were determined to print their own books. In this way they hoped to cut out the frustration of working with various publishers and not quite being allowed to say exactly what they wanted to in their books. Their writing became moderately successful, and it seemed as if Roger and Annalie could look forward to a very pleasant retirement. They started traveling and speaking in order to help sales of their books, but soon Annalie had to give this up because she was becoming increasingly arthritic. Through their work they knew that they needed certain energies to cure arthritis and they did their best to reinforce Annalie's spirit with the proper energies; but she became more and more troubled by the disease until one time when Roger came back from a month-long tour he found she was hardly able to walk. This spelt disaster, of course; both in Annalie's life and in the secure retirement they had arranged for themselves. For if Annalie was immobilized, Roger could not leave her to travel. Further he felt that without her, life would be meaningless.

They turned to us for aid. The first thing we did was to

instruct them to change Annalie's diet and to include in it many of the red, acid fruits that really help people with arthritis. Then we told them, instead of sending healing energies at any old time, to send them only when Aries was overhead.

Annalie recovered quickly with this treatment; after six months or so she again relapsed. This called for a further analysis of the total situation. It turned out that the basic problem was this: Annalie was torturing her body by sitting hour after hour motionless at a composer-keyboard retyping the book manuscripts which they printed in their business. This constant lack of motion meant that her joints were simply freezing up. No amount of healing energy could overcome such abuse of the body. They hired a girl to carry the typing load. Roger started, gently at first, making Annalie walk; he forbade her to sit either in a wheelchair or on her castered typing chair. Thus she was forced to stand up and walk. Gradually this treatment, together with the healing energies, wrought a permanent cure.

Selecting Your Cosmic Hour and Conducting a Healing

We learn from Annalie's case, as we did from Walt's, that many factors affect the body. Annalie was a normally healthy, vibrant woman; yet because she sat in one position for hours upon end, she damaged her body and it reacted with the disease of arthritis.

When you attempt a cure, it is easy to decide which healing energy you need. You can get that directly from your Cosmic Healing Wheel. To make the cure permanent, you must establish what is causing the unbalance. Is it basic nature? Home pressures? Job pressures? Pressures from the peer group? And you must remove this pressure from the patient. As you learned from Chapter III, every day energies from every part of the cosmos are available to you. If you want to heal someone, you must select a time for that healing attempt which utilizes this eternal natural rhythm of energy.

If you wish to lay hands on someone and direct cosmic energy into his spirit, for instance, more of the appropriate cosmic energy is available when the proper segment of the Wheel for curing the illness in question is directly overhead. Looking at Figure III-1, you see that each day all the specific types of energy from the cosmos are at maximum when you are directly beneath them and the energy is not coming in either slantwise or having to reach you through part of the earth. The graph Figure V-3 shows this effect. It also shows quite clearly that you have several hours in which to accomplish your healing work when each energy is at a maximum. Of course it is useless just to sit and passively hope that these energies will do you some good. You must constantly work at the problem. Sometimes it takes many days of using these energies to effect a cure.

To cure yourself, you visualize yourself into the animal representing the energies you need for the two hours or so the energies are available to you. To cure others, you first visualize yourself into the animal form at the correct time of day, and then lay your hands on the afflicted part and visualize the energy flowing into the patient's body. If the pa-

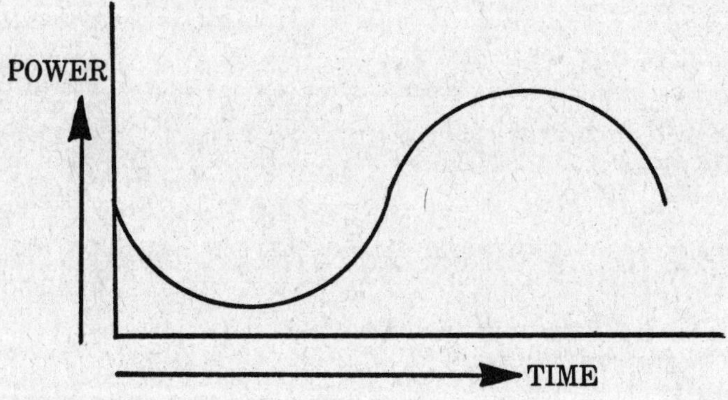

Graph shows variation with time of the power from one area of the heavens due to the earth's shadow.

Figure V-3
Power Available

tient is cooperative and will not resist your suggestions, you can additionally encourage him to wear the appropriate sign from Table I-1.

Bless Thyself with Eternal Youth and Good Health

Inshallah! The world, the cosmos, is wondrous in its manifest parts . . . . everything in it hath its place, its use, and its meaning. Thou blasphemest thy Maker if thou dost not take care of the temple of thy body. Equally thou dost commit a grievous error if thou dost not keep thy spirit in balance. Didst thou ever recognize that when thou dost not live life to the fullest and use all the faculties, delights, and forces at thy command, thou art equally blaspheming thy Maker? He did not put these faculties and delights at thy disposal so that thou shouldst ignore them.

Some healthy persons do rant and rave at thee that thou shouldst not dance or drink wine or make love. In His time the great Prophet himself did warn against the drinking of wine. But knowing the weakness of men, He did not make the penalty for drinking wine overly grievous; and thus the people of my land still do benefit from the blessings of a full rounded life. Hast thou not seen the merchant who still in the fullness of his life and the enjoyment of his trade doth allow his son to succeed him? And upon his son's assured succession doth wither and die like unto the overripe fruit on the vine? Thou mayest look with longing toward thy retirement from what thou perceivest as the evil of work; but I say unto thee that as surely as night doth follow day, death will follow thy retirement if thou dost at thy retirement relinquish the activities which thy body hath grown accustomed to. It is e'en so that if thou dost retire from the delights of the world before thy time, thou wilt lose thy vigor and die.

Keep thy body in balance. Use all thy faculties. Make love to thy wives; enjoy thy concubines. Grow thy crops; or if it be thy path, compete freely with the other merchants. Thou wilt be assured of youthful vigor until thy dying day.

Ailing Seymour Becomes a Vital New Corporate President

Student File 3Y-2RM

Seymour H was a typical young man about town. His father, Martin, had made a fortune in upholstery fabrics in New York City. The relationship between Martin and Seymour was a close one because Seymour's mother had died when he was still a young child. The two loves of Martin's life were his business and Seymour. He spent every waking moment on one or the other. Consequently Seymour had all the money he wished to spend—and did in fact do his best to spend it. Martin didn't really object to this; he was fond of saying, "He's living the life I would have led at his age if I'd had any money." Martin always resisted Seymour's requests to let him come in and learn the business. "You're only young once," and similar responses were Martin's reply to Seymour's offers of participation.

Gradually the purposeless life that Seymour led took its toll. First he broke his ankle on the ski slopes of Mont Tremblant; this was followed by a series of minor ailments, all of which exacted a price from both Seymour and Martin. While Seymour was hospitalized, he became interested in our course; and fairly soon began to think about his disabilities in a new way. He realized that in order to balance his life he would have to get a job. As soon as he was able, while his ankle was still in a cast, he approached his father on the subject. Martin refused to give him a job, even the most menial one in the business. He could not see that Seymour really needed to work to balance his life. Finally father and son had the first serious quarrel of their family life. Seymour made up his mind to go out to the west coast and prove to Martin that he could indeed make it in the business world. He found that this was not as easy as he had anticipated, though he did have a good talent for selling. After he had been on the west coast for some time and was beginning to be successful, he got a call from Herschel, Martin's factory manager, to say that Martin had been rushed to the hospital, and could Seymour come in to take charge of things? Seymour took the next flight east. He went straight to the hospital, where Martin assured him of his own immediate return to work, and urged him not to get too involved.

With Herschel's tutelage Seymour quickly learned the basics of the business. He found that his west coast experience was very useful in dealing with the customers, and that the running of day-to-day matters could be left to Herschel.

At Seymour's return from the coast, Martin recovered rapidly, and with his recovery tried to take over his former role in the business; however, the fact that Seymour had demonstrated such good capabilities and was obviously far healthier and happier than he had been when he was living in enforced idleness made Martin reconsider his previous insistence that Seymour act the part of a playboy and 'enjoy' himself—on Martin's terms.

Father and son worked well together in the business, though Herschel had to be the buffer while they worked out their precedents. The lightening of the load on Martin and the new happy relationship with his son put fresh life into the old man.

Since Martin now had more time to himself, Seymour encouraged him to get *his* life fully rounded. This became a fairy story in the making. Martin met an attractive widow, Susannah, and fell head over heels for her. Becky, her only daughter, had an equal impact on Seymour. Martin took his new bride off on a world cruise, while Seymour stayed at home with Becky to run the business. While in Scotland, Martin got involved in the production aspects of some of the finer woolen fabrics and felt that he would like to start a new business in this field. At the young age of 55 he is now the president of a small exclusive woolen fabrics concern, and Seymour is running the old business, having quite overcome all the ailments he had while he was just acting the playboy. Because Martin's new business is not really a full-time occupation, he and Susannah do a great deal of traveling and enjoy the jet-set activities available in Europe. The last time we heard from these friends, they had what they referred to as a "reverse generation gap" going. Martin has become the swinger and Seymour is the hard-working businessman. Our last letter warned them most seriously that they could overbalance in this direction too; whether or not they took any notice of the warning we don't know, for we have not heard from them for several years.

Putting the Knowledge of This Chapter to Work for You

To proceed with any healing, you need before you the Cosmic Healing Wheel shown in Figure V-2, the timing device from Figure III-1, and the appropriate animal representations for each segment of the heavens which will produce the energies you need. Let us now review the steps you will take to accomplish a healing.

1. Establish the root cause of the dis-ease.* (The visible symptoms of the dis-ease do not necessarily indicate its true cause). It is up to you to identify the cause and correct it, so that the dis-ease will indeed be cured. You must not just cover up a symptom with these techniques, as you might paint over a damp spot in a house you wanted to sell; you must persist until the actual root cause is corrected. You must, shall we say, prevent the damp coming into the house, not just paint over it. When you have established the cause of the dis-ease, then you can proceed to Step 2.

2. In the life of the patient, make the necessary changes which will bring in energies of a different segment of the heavens. Remember how Nicholas made the children dance the dance of an animal that would help them. By using the techniques given in Chapter I, you can bring these energies in on a continuous basis.

3. When you have a severe case on your hands, you must add your own energies tuned to the correct animal nature to those that you have been able to bring into the life of the

*Editor: Sic.

patient. To do this most effectively, you should do it when the correct segment of the Heavenly Wheel is over your head. By calculating from the dawn time as you were taught to do in Chapter III, you can tell when this occurs.

4. No cure is complete unless the body is fully repaired. The body may need medication, herbs, and foods that you do not have available. It is always wise, therefore, to have an orthodox physician prescribe these things for a patient. The physician is prescribing for the body; you are prescribing for the spirit. The two go hand in hand; they are complementary procedures. Doing both assures a more rapid recovery than doing either one by itself.

Mighty Works Require a Perfect Body

With the aid of this book you are hopefully on the threshold of changing your whole life. Soon now if you follow our procedures you will be stepping into a new you with a brighter future. The importance of good health is thus twofold: (1) Not only must you now be healthy so that you can carry out your campaign and overcome every obstacle; but (2) once you have overcome these obstacles you must be healthy to enjoy the fruits of your victory. The procedures to gain health are easy. They will take you just a few minutes a day.

It may be that you are inherently healthy but that friends around you drag you down with their health problems. In order to succeed, you must be able to proceed to your work with a clear mind and a healthy body. Thus you should cure your friends so that they will not take from your energy. Many people put up with minor ill health and allow it to sap their energies without really knowing exactly what is wrong with them. There is really no excuse for this type of foolishness. A competent doctor can usually diagnose quickly any ailment you may have. If he cannot, then a trusted psychic should be able to help. For the psychic will tell you the ills of your spirit, which after all are reflected and manifest themselves as ills of the body.

Chapter Six

THE ASTROMANTIC SECRET OF GAINING FRIENDS AND AFFECTION

What This Chapter Will Do for You

Are you lonely? Do you sometimes feel left out of it at parties? The wallflower at a dance? This chapter will correct all those problems for you and will fill your life with new friends and acquaintances.

Westerners Are Lonely People

In the time in which I lived, great sultans did rule vast areas of the world known then. They sent forth armies and conquered their enemies. When war was over and peace did return, all returned to their appointed places in the village in which they were born. A few, it is true, moved to work with relatives in the grandeur of a city; but oftentimes methinks they did soon tire of this glittering life, so that many did return again unto their villages. For in the village they knew their place—even if that place might be considered lowly. In thy world, people move into the glamor and glitter of the cities in search of employment in vast concerns, concerns that dwarf even the rug-makers' consortium of ancient Persia. Few of these success-seekers realize what they trade for this glitter and glamor. Life-long friends are cast aside. Family ties are broken asunder. The poor lonely seeker after a caliph's treasure doth find only loneliness with his success. As he climbeth the ladder of progress and becometh more powerful, so doth the loneliness increase. The great wealth consisting of the friendships of this life is for ever lost, especially when thou gainest the jewels and gold of a sultan. For always wilt thou ask thyself, "Why cometh this man to see me? What doth he hope to gain?" Nevertheless, e'en in my time some were lonely; and the Watchers did put their minds to the task of improving the lot of these poor lonely souls. The rules they did develop are as sound today as ever they were. Thou needest not be lonely, for e'en in the large crowd of a city there are other persons who have natures like unto thine own and will be thy friends.

Even as the grains of sand in the desert are each individual and different, so it is in the city. When the wind doth blow, it sorteth the grains so that the larger fall in one place and the smaller in another. E'en as the winds blow in the desert, so do the travels and flows of men in the city sort them into groups. What thou must do is find thy group. If thou art shy and retiring, thou canst not readily venture into the flow of people; thus thou wilt for ever be lonely. Or, what is far far worse, thou wilt meet another lonely soul and marry to overcome thy loneliness rather than for love. If thou art retiring and placest thyself not in the path of the winds that blow in one direction and another, thou art like unto a grain of sand caught in a box. Thou must go out and let the wind take thee where it will; for only in this way wilt thou meet souls like unto thyself. When thou goest to a party and findest thyself next to an individual who might be to thy liking, thou must draw near and speak if thou art to break out of thy prison.

Shy, Aimless George Gains Direction and Friendship

Student File 2Y-4LQ

George K joined our School when he became partially paralyzed after a tangle with a rambunctious steer on his father's farm in Arkansas. George could get about with the aid of a good strong stick, but his walk was always slow and a little awkward. He went back to the home of his parents but could do little to help on the farm; and because everyone around him was very active, he felt terribly alone and useless. One day he saw an ad in the paper for the UN, who wanted farm advisers for some of the third-world nation programs. Now George was no slouch mentally, and he had a good degree in agriculture from Minneapolis; so he had no difficulty in getting one of the positions the UN was offering. He moved to New York and even with his slow walk found no difficulty in going to many theaters and movies, and even around several of the museums.

It took George several months to realize how alone he was. With his slight physical handicap and natural country reticence, he really had no friends. On the weekends he found himself sitting in the window of his apartment watching small groups of youngsters and couples wander by, and began to feel tremendously left out and cheated by the world. He even gave up his work on our course and stopped bothering to explore the available pleasures of the big city. He became an embittered recluse.

All these negative feelings came to a head in him one Sunday night which happened to be the third of July. In those days we occasionally let our students call us by telephone, and George, feeling very suicidal, did just that. He talked to us at long-distance rates for nearly two hours. Basically he got nearly all the negative feelings out of his head by laying them on us. When he had finished his diatribe against the world and against whatever universal god had caused his trouble, we were able to guide him gently into a more positive frame of mind about himself and about what his future might bring. We pointed out that his suicidal feelings and loneliness were probably brought about by the fact that here it was Sunday night, the time on the farm for a party, and not only that, but tomorrow should be a family day, the Fourth of July, a day when friends and family gathered from miles around to whoop it up. Then we told him about the problems of his nature, which was that of a Virgo, home-loving and relatively retiring.

We suggested he might try thinking about what life would be like if instead of being born a Virgo he had been born a Gemini. He protested strongly for several minutes that his nature was unchangeable. After several more minutes we convinced him that he could at least act out the part of someone with a different nature. Eventually we convinced him to go to the UN's American delegation party on the following day and while there to be a flibberti-gibbet magpie. We even gave him a few rather corny Gemini-type jokes to crack. About midnight we finally convinced him he could do it, and hung up the phone.

The next night a jubilant George reported that it worked. We could hear sounds of talking and revelry in the background, so we asked him where he was. "Why, in my apartment of course. A bunch of the people came back with me and we're having a good old-fashioned hootnanny right here in the middle of the city."

Bring the Warmth and Direction of the Desert Winds to Your Heart

You can follow George's example and Ibn Saud's direction very easily. In any large city or community you will find associations or clubs or societies where people of similar natures gather. This is particularly true of immigrants from Europe who overcome their loneliness by forming old-country clubs; though with care and a little searching, you will find the same type of clubs for American geographical areas and for special-interest groups. A glance at the telephone directory of any large city will show you that there are more of these groups than you have dreamed existed. They are the result of what Ibn Saud would call the 'desert winds' pushing and sorting individuals. By nature you may be quiet, shy and retiring as George was; but as you learned in preceding chapters of this book, you can change your nature.

Ibn Saud clearly advised us that the natures into which one should change are those associated with the wind. These are the 'air signs.' They are the heavenly segments of Gemini, Libra, and Aquarius; and each exhibits an affectionate nature that is easy to get along with. Within these three signs, however, there are subtle differences. The Gemini (Magpie) is the one who does not form deep friendships, for it flits around. The Libra (Swan) forms more lasting attachments of a romantic nature. The Aquarius (Phoenix) forms lasting attachments of the hail-fellow-well-met type or finds fulfillment as 'one of the girls.' You need only take on one of these 'wind of the desert' characteristics, and without effort you can gain a whole raft of new acquaintances, provided only that you go out and mingle with the crowds.

Table VI-1 specifies precisely which birth months are related to which elements. From this table you can see, for instance, that one whose birthdate is listed in the Fire column will find compatible friends from birthdates in that same column.

Using the Astromantic Laws of Attraction and Complementarity

When the Watchers of ancient time did record the characteristics of the various natures of man, they did find that some, as we have said, were like the warm winds of the desert; they ascribed to these an airy nature. Today these are called the air signs. Others they found had a nature like unto that of water, which doth run easily around obstacles and always findeth its own level. Others they did assign to the mother of life, earth. These natures, let it be said, are very fixed, earthy, rooted. Some might even call them uninteresting; but they are forsooth the most solid and reliable of our people. Last, to lend spice to the dullness of life, there are those natures which are like unto the fire. Verily they brighten the intellect and lend to life an explosive character that by its nature maketh all others seem bland. Now if thou art of a nature like water, thou shouldst not make a friend of someone who is of the fire; for when water and fire try to mix, naught but disaster occurreth. Similarly, when air and water do try to mix, the only result is a rain squall.

Fire	Air	Earth	Water
Aries— Ram	Gemini— Magpie	Taurus— Bull	Cancer— Crab
Leo— Lion	Libra— Swan	Virgo— Virgin Maiden	Scorpio— Scorpion
Sagittarius— Centaur	Aquarius— Phoenix	Capricorn— Goat	Pisces— Fish

Table VI-1
Table of Elemental Natures

I hear that these four natures are now called 'elements.' If thou seekest to make a friend of an acquaintance thou hast met, thou must first learn exactly what nature thy acquaintance hath before making him a friend; for if his nature is opposed to thine, naught can come of it. Oft hath it been said that opposites attract one another, that in sooth they complement one another; however, Allah hath decreed that the Law of Attraction ruleth thy life more directly than doth the Law of Complementarity. This meaneth that for a stable and happy life thou shouldst make close friends only of those who are of thy nature. For be assured that although a nature that is different from thine is interesting to explore, still as time doth progress on its continuing round, exploration will cease and annoyance and friction will result from the insurmountable differences that are present in incompatible natures. Ferocious are the storms and sad are the wrecked lives that do result from these incompatibilities of natures. Those storms and wrecks could be avoided if people did but understand the basic cosmic laws that govern life. There should be no blame attached to these storms; but emotion doth too often govern, and rational, enduring friendships are the exception, not the rule.

Edgar and Candy's Disastrous Marriage Could Have Been Avoided

Student File 2G-1PV

Candy L was born in the month of Gemini. We were never able to get her to study properly; her nature was much too light and flighty for the work we asked her to do. In the hope of helping her, we introduced her to another student Edgar, who was a good solid Capricorn. He was an excellent student, somewhat older than Candy, and had been studying the Craft for many years as a solitary Witch. Thus we were partly responsible for the disaster we brought into the life of Edgar and Candy.

The first time Edgar met Candy, he fell head over heels in love with her. For him it was love at first sight. Her nature, of course, was such that she happily went out with him. Her life was as the air: easily directed and controlled; and in working with Edgar as well as dating him, she at least temporarily showed a little seriousness and thus for a short time she gave up her airy magpie flighty habits. In her way she came to depend on Edgar, and she probably thought this was love. Edgar's infatuation continued to grow stronger day by day. Soon they came to us and asked to be handfasted; but because they had not lived together for a year and a day as our tradition requires, we refused. This did not prevent them from getting married by a local judge. I suppose our biggest feeling at the time was one of frustration, for all our instincts told us that we were witnessing the makings of a minor tragedy. However they stayed together for nearly three years before Candy, feeling totally stifled and ensnared, started flitting around the town again. She meant little by it; she was a completely faithful wife. What she needed was companionship and friendship and people she could chatter with. Edgar, however, in his serious business way, and being older and therefore having less energy, could not understand her needs. Thus he became more and more unhappy. We told him to try and change, and for short periods he did become the Gemini and go the rounds with Candy. But, probably because of his age, he could not keep it up; and eventually they ended in the divorce court.

Your Astromantic Friendship Dial

In order to make it easy for you to find people who have the same nature as yourself, and who you can be sure will return to you friendship for friendship, we have for several years been using the Law of Attraction of the elements that Ibn Saud explained. Since everything in nature is cyclical, this too is made up as the circular dial shown in Figure VI-1. All you have to do is place the small dial over the larger dial and clip them together. Then you can immediately see the birthdates of people who will be of your element. Those of like elements, of course, are those that you can be sure will make good friends. If you have many acquaintances, it is a matter of but a few moments to find out which ones will repay your investment in friendship and which ones are incompatible. Notice particularly the dotted line and arrowhead. This signifies what Ibn Saud called the Law of Complementarity. For a short time, maybe even a few years, people who are in this time period will make good friends for you; however, these friendships too often end in heartbreak, sorrow, and bitterness.

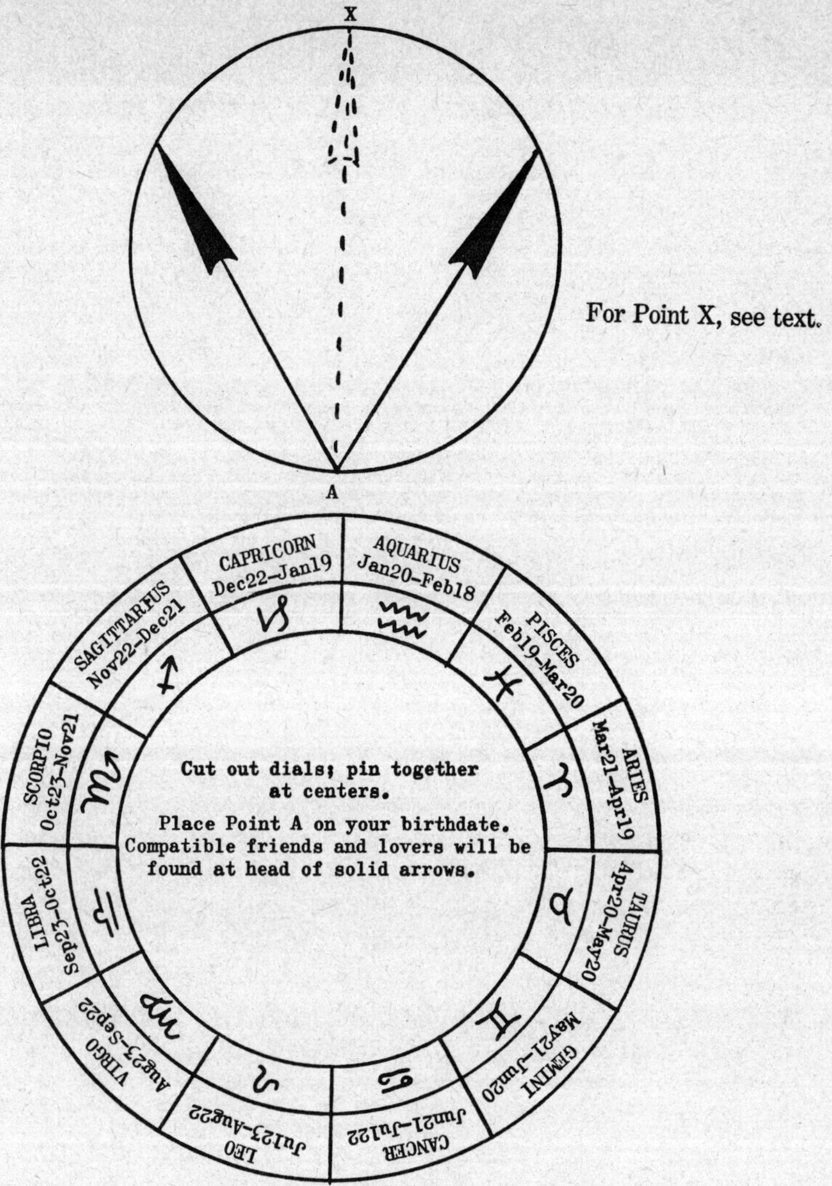

Figure VI-1
Your Astromantic Friendship Dial

The Tempering of Your Friendship

In thy youth thou hadst many acquaintances; and in thy common battle against parents and others who did direct thy life, thou didst grow close to these acquaintances and they became life-long friends. Why is it, thou mayest ask, that even though these friends have many diverse natures and do not correspond to any single element, still they are thy friends and even until thy death will so remain? Many years ago in Persia I was with a caravan train that was attacked by a band of robbing hawks from the desert. We did beat back those marauding robbers and did after much bloodshed and trouble triumph both over this adversary and the adversity they caused; for in the skirmish much of the train's water was lost and many reached the next oasis with swollen tongues and cracked lips. For many years after, when men from that caravan train came to my small village they came to see me and I gladly allowed them to partake of what small fare I had. I offered them a place to rest their head and the pleasures of my serving girls. Many times when I visited another village I went out of my way to find a comrade from that caravan. We were friends. We were friends unto the death for we had been tempered together in the same fire and our elemental natures became melded. When thou heatest the grains of sand from the desert in a furnace, thou comest out with glass; the grains have joined one with another until they are henceforth indistinguishable and inseparable. Thus when thou hast a friend, like the good smith tempering a sword thou must temper the friendship with adversity so that the diverse elements can be brought together. If thou dost depend for thy life on an untried friend, thou art the most foolish of men.

The great sages of the past in their work found that life-endangering adversity was not the only way in which divergent natures could be melded. They found that if different natures were taken through a complete cycle of the elements:

fire, earth, air, and water, what had previously been different could be harmonized, provided only that the people so harmonized were born not more than 39 moon-cycles apart.

Joe, Al, and Frank Make Barney a Friend

Joe, Al, and Frank were tenth-grade teenagers in one of our local schools. Frank's cousin Barney came to the school in mid-semester when his father was transferred to a plant in town. Frank introduced his cousin to his other friends, and Barney naturally joined the trio, making it a foursome instead of a threesome. Barney just didn't fit in, though. When the other three were united in doing something or playing a prank, or dating a particular group of girls, Barney always seemed to be the one who objected to doing that thing at this particular time. When they got into minor scrapes, it always seemed to be Barney who let the group down. Consequently Barney was gradually ostracized; and because he was ostracized from one group in the tenth grade, he could not seem to find another group who would take him in. The need for peer-group recognition, though he would not have called it that, really affected Barney's work. His constant cry, "I don't have any friends," fell on deaf ears when report-card time rolled around. "That's all the more reason you should do good school work," said his father.

Because he was lonely Barney got interested in a superficial way in the occult and in Witchcraft. Fortunately his father was well versed in these arts and sciences, and directed his son's reading into positive channels. Of course, Frank soon heard of Barney's interest, and then Al and Joe also heard of it. Thinking it would be a prank, the three conned Barney into doing a ritual for them. Barney was quite concerned at what he had gotten into and sensibly talked with his father about it. His father advised him to do a friendship ritual; for by doing this he would not only show his acquaintances that he was knowledgeable and skilled, but also that there was truth in the occult sciences. Barney and his father worked up a little new-moon ritual to be performed at high noon. The boys were disappointed at this, because they had hoped to do something spooky in the middle of the night by the light of the moon. But things done at new moon grow; and since it was a friendship growth Barney wanted, he was correct in selecting a new-moon ritual.

At the appointed time, with all sorts of strange words, Barney cast a circle around himself and his friends. He shook feathers, rang bells, beat gongs, all this merely to impress his friends and put on a show. Then he had each friend take off his shoes and step into a bowl of water with him. Next he made each one step over a fire three times. Then he had each give him a little hair and a small nail-clipping. He bound these bits of nail and hair with some of his own, and burned them in the fire. Then he had each lad turn over a small spadeful of earth. From the spadeful Barney took a pinch, shook it with water, and made them drink.

Barney never again had trouble melding his and his friends' wishes. They were now one in friendship, a friendship that endured through school and into the college years.

There Is No Physical Danger in Astromantic Friendship Bonding

What Barney did was to expose his friends to each of the four elements while they were within the confines of an Astromantic circle. Since his friends were of the same age as he was, they were all affected in an identical way by being made, for instance, to stand in a bowl of water together. Similarly when they stepped over fire and formed fumes (air) by burning hair and nail-clippings, they were facing together each element in turn. They were not exposed (except perhaps in their own minds) to any real stress. Yes, they jointly shared a secret; but the key to the success of the procedure was their joint exposure to each element in turn.

Tempering an Acquaintance into a Friend

When you have an acquaintance whom you are absolutely sure you would like to turn into a good friend, you can accomplish this with a procedure similar to the one Barney undertook. We have found that it will work best if the friend is present with you in the circle and if you are both undressed for the ritual. It should of course be done at noon on a day when the moon is new. All you need to do is cast a circle in salt with a radius of 2.72 feet around a central hearthstone in which you have kindled a small fire. Once you are both inside, you should psychically close the circle with an affirmation like this one:

> "We are surrounded by the pure white light of the Gods. Nothing but good can come to us; nothing but good can go from us."

Stand together in a large container of water in the western part of the circle. Face the east and say,

> "We two friends ask you Undines of the waters that our minds be joined so that they are as one."

Next stand to the north of the fire and face south. Say,

> "Great Salamanders and spirits of the south, join our temperaments so that they are as one."

Step forward and backward across the fire three times in unison with an arm around each other's waist.

Now face to the west with the fire between you and the western point of the circle. Say,

> "Gnomes of the west, we ask that you make our capabilities and our bodies as one."

From a glass of water to which you have added a pinch of soil, drink a sip. Facing then to the north, with the fire between you and the north, cast into the fire a small package containing a few hair clippings from each of your heads and a few nail clippings from each one's fingers. Say,

> "Sylphs of the north, we ask that our emotions be as one. As the airs from products of our bodies ascend to you, we ask that you make us as one."

Now stand one on each side of the fire, with hands joined across it. Say,

> "God above and goddess below, we pray you: Grant our wish.
> We thank you for your presence and for the presence of your servants.
> We will honor you in all our thoughts and actions.
> Undines, Salamanders, Gnomes, and Sylphs: Depart you now in peace."

It is usual now for the partners to embrace over the fire and to leave the circle at its easternmost point with another affirmation like the following:

> "We carry with us our circle of protection and bonding. The power we have shall go into our bond and reinforce it."

Dovetailing the Astromagic

Many students have tried unsuccessfully to do friendship circles with people who were totally unsuited to be their friends. If you brought your enemy and placed him in a circle with you and did all the friendship circles in the world you might finally turn his head around far enough so that he would become your friend; but it would be a long and arduous procedure—and when you were all through, all you would have would be a bird caged by your rituals. It is very likely that eventually the bird would break out of the cage anyway and hate you even more for having caged it.

To find friends, you must first have many acquaintances. To get acquaintances, you must emulate and copy air-sign characteristics. Once you have a large group of acquaintances, you can select the ones who are most likely to be good friends. Your selection process must not be based on outward looks, but be done Astromagically by selecting the underlying spirits, the very essential nature of each acquaintance whom you wish to become a friend. Remember too the 39-moon rule. Do not try to force a friendship onto someone whose birthdate is more than three years and three months away from your own. Yes, of course, you can force friendship on any acquaintance as you could on an enemy; but again: The work is very arduous, and when the chips are down the magic may break. Use the Astromantic dial in Figure VI-1 first before you work the friendship ritual. Once you have selected those acquaintances whom you wish to make your friends, it is a simple matter to share an elemental friendship ritual.

Gwen Loses Her Car but Gains a Friend

Student File 2G-7KS

Gwen L lives in Boston, Massachusetts. She came to live there from a small town in upstate New York. She had always heard of Boston as a cultural center, and after the death of her parents came there so that she could taste the cultural delights which she had so much lacked in her home town. Being of a Pisces nature, she was always looking for mystery and always believed in her heart of hearts that whatever she willed, would happen. When she first came to Boston, to save on expenses she shared an apartment with Bobbie W, who was a graduate of Vassar. Somehow the slight snobbery that Bobbie displayed appealed to Gwen. Her Pisces nature was quite content to let Bobbie (by nature a Scorpio) dominate her life.

Then Bobbie married. She and Norm found a house they liked in Cambridge, signed the papers to buy it, and moved in. At the last moment, though, the bank turned down their application for a loan. Bobbie went to her old friend Gwen with a request to cosign the note; Gwen readily agreed. Within two weeks, Norm eloped to Mexico with a dancer from a local night spot, leaving Bobbie—and Gwen—holding the bag. A couple of months went by, and Bobbie accepted a new roommate into the house for which Gwen had cosigned; he was a college student without funds.

At Norm's departure, Bobbie had stopped making payments on the mortgage. Now the bank turned to Gwen to make them good. She made a payment or two, but in this manner became liable legally for the remainder. Now Bobbie and her student roommate packed up and vacated the house, telling Gwen they intended to let the bank have it back to sell again. Gwen was aghast. She could see her credit rating plummeting and her budget plans destroyed by the enormous house payments she had committed herself to make. Moreover, when she went to the house, she found in every room the evidence of wild parties and enthusiastic love-ins. She foresaw thousands of dollars worth of repair before the house could be regarded as saleable.

When all the flack and fury died down, Gwen found herself on the line for a bill she could not pay. Gwen's upbringing did not allow her to renege on her commitment, so she sold her dearly beloved antique Cadillac to get the house into marketable condition. She was furious—as furious as a Pisces can get—about the situation, and she wrote to us for a spell to fix Bobbie. After reviewing the whole thing with Gwen over several months, we concluded that what Gwen really wanted was Bobbie's continued friendship. Gwen was just lonely, and was frustrated that she had put so much into a friendship that had turned sour.

We told Gwen to do a circle friendship ritual using Bobbie's picture. As Gwen stepped out of the circle she had cast in her apartment living room, the telephone was ringing. It was Bobbie. She wished to move back in with Gwen and somehow make amends.

The friendship that was magically started and melded has carried on through both girls' marriages, and they are still as firmly cemented together as they ever were: both because of the ritual and by the fact that they were inherently compatible to begin with. Gwen's Pisces and Bobbie's Scorpio were on the compatibility line of the Astromantic friendship wheel, and the girls were of similar ages. Thus the friendship circle worked for them as it can for you any time you try it, provided you are careful to make the original choice of acquaintances with care.

Fire, Earth, Air, Water: the Elements Control Friendship

Over the many years since Ibn Saud enumerated the laws which govern basic friendships, we have not only experimented with his system, but have also found that those laws were not as lost as he had thought; for many modern astrologers knew of them. Something even newer has been added by these astrologers, for they have found one fire-water relationship which is also compatible—that of Aries and Scorpio. Since we have lost contact with Ibn Saud, we have no explanation for this and we have never found an explanation from the astrologers whom we have asked for it. Put it into your bag of magical procedures, though; for it is one which works.

Find your acquaintances, classify them, pick your friends. Magically, Astromantically, cement these friendships together. They will endure forever.

Chapter Seven

ASTROMANTICALLY SATISFYING THE ROMANTIC NEEDS OF A SHEIK

What This Chapter Can Do for You

Finding romance among your friends is oftentimes difficult. This chapter will not only show you how to find romance; it will also show you how to:

- Fulfill your romantic needs without emotional entanglement
- Find your twin soul
- Bring understanding into your marriage
- Assure that your marriage will be long-lasting and full of love
- Teach you how to break away from an unsuitable partner

Completing the Balance of Your Life with Romance

Art thou complete in thy life? Or art thou romantically unfulfilled and unbalanced? Allah made thee a complete being. Just as He made the Wheel of the Heavens above thy head complete, so He gave thee senses, emotions, and drives. If in thy life thou dost suppress any of these composite parts of thy nature, thou art like unto a wheel which lacketh a spoke. Such a wheel runneth not true, nor is it of use even for a rope to run over to draw water from the well. It causeth naught but trouble.

Some men have fear of showing their true nature. Others have been told that the great God useth our nature to tempt us to evil. My child, I have studied the sayings and the writings men have made since ancient time. I can tell thee truly that there is naught in the holy books to deny true health-giving affection between those of opposite sex, provided only that they are not committed to another and that their ultimate bodily blending doth not defile the law of nature. Do not trust men who tell thee 'thou shalt not,' for they wish only to control thee. It is assuredly true that when a caravan crosseth the desert the caravan-master must promulgate certain laws. The caravan must not have within its ranks dissension; for if it doth, when the desert vultures attack and attempt to rob it, it will not act as one. But when the caravan is out of danger these laws should be trampled in the sand. Is it not true that when Moses and his band of refugees fled the wrath of Pharaoh they did for their own benefit abide by certain laws? But when the great prophet Jesus and his lord the beloved Mohammed, Allah akbar, came unto this earth, then all the holy books agree that those who accept them have no need to follow the law of Moses. Doth not even the Christian guide book say, "Christ hath redeemed us from the curse of the law."[1]

---

[1]Galatians III:13

At other times and in other places leaders have promulgated laws that curbed and confined men, denying them their natures. Many churches forbade their leaders the comfort of marriage; for they were afraid lest if their leaders married they would give their profit not unto the church but unto their natural kinfolk. I say unto thee: Thou must in the correct time of thy life experience all the fruits of the senses thou hast been given. To deny the senses is to deny that Allah Himself existeth and hath made thee whole.

Paul Overcomes Pain with Romance

Paul L lived in Santa Fe, New Mexico. His had been a happy marriage, though there were no children. After his retirement and the death of his wife, Paul felt he now had little to live for. Slowly he seemed to fade away. He himself often thought that if he were to die, no one would even notice he was gone, let alone mourn his passing.

All this changed when he met Lavinia at a Santa Fe supermarket. She too was alone in this world; she too was widowed; and she was just a couple of years younger than Paul. Paul felt some of the old stirrings of love in his blood and bones, and began to court Lavinia in earnest. He felt that Lavinia was returning his affection and that in fact she too was looking forward to the time when they could be united. Only one obstacle lay in their way: Paul was a Catholic and Lavinia was a Baptist. As adult human beings, they decided they would visit Paul's priest and Lavinia's minister to get their opinions on the forthcoming match. Fortunately or unfortunately—we cannot say which—the strain of waiting was too strong for this fond couple, and a few nights before their appointments with the priest and the minister they consummated their relationship.

Paul shocked Lavinia to her very core when he quite matter-of-factly told the priest what had happened. The priest passed this off, though he insisted rather strongly that Paul should pay a penance for it. Further the priest said that he could not encourage a mixed marriage. Lavinia was not so straightforward with her minister as Paul had been with the priest, but still the minister got the message and started off on a full-fledged diatribe against the sin of fornication. Paul just didn't want to hear it, so he got up and left; this further annoyed Lavinia. When Paul visited her that evening, she told him she had made up her mind she never wanted to see him again. In his anger Paul agreed with her. Such words as 'narrow-minded' and 'bigoted' were exchanged.

Paul shut himself off from the world and once more started the downward slide into ill health and senility which would lead to death. While he had been out and about with Lavinia, he had picked up several new books, for in his earlier life he had been a voracious reader. One of these was our "Witch's Guide to Life." As he told us afterward, it was as though a light had come on in his head and he realized how other people had been trying to control him all his life.

Ten years later, Paul is still going strong. He has not married yet, but his latest 'friend' has been with him for several years; and it does look as though one of these days they will legalize the relationship they both enjoy. Paul is in the best of health, of course, as is his lady. They are not consumed by any thoughts that they are committing some 'sin' and they have plenty of life left to live.

Health Balances Romance on the Wheel of Life

As Ibn Saud directed us, all the areas of your life should be in balance. Of course Paul grew sickly by keeping romance and love out of his life. We constantly see in younger people cases of high emotion, skin disease, and ulcers that are magically cured as soon as they find romance. The problem is that for centuries people have been controlled through their senses and have come to believe what they are told. Nowadays, fortunately, young people are coming to recognize that those controls are meaningless—and in fact cause both mental and physical sickness.

Only rarely in time past were people able to throw off

those yokes. On one such occasion in the 14th Century, the Bishop of Orkney was finally murdered by his exasperated congregation because he had decreed that those who married even fourth or fifth cousins were sinners. He brandished his Latin Bible (which no one in the Orkneys could read) and through his laws confiscated some 60 percent of the land. When a new Earl of Orkney was appointed by the King of Norway, he forthrightly told the islanders that he too could read the book and the bishop had lied; for the book forbade marriages only between first cousins. Thus the bishop died through trying to enslave the island people and steal their land.

Are you being enslaved and made ill by someone else's rules—rules that you don't agree with? Or are you properly balanced, so that, having experienced all, you can control all?

Let us look for a moment at another evil (for we define ignorance as evil): the child who is brought up in total ignorance of alcohol. Having no skill in handling alcohol, the young person takes too much of it, perhaps at a party; not knowing what he is doing, he loses control of his faculties, makes a fool of himself, and winds up in jail—or worse: on the highway has an accident that takes many lives. Would it not be better for the child to learn to deal with alcohol and its effects under the loving guidance of his parents before being turned loose? In this manner he would be able prudently to use it or decline it; his training would have equipped him with the knowledge necessary for judicious behavior.

Using the Trine of Love to Bring Romance into Your Life Astromantically

By following the steps outlined below, you can automatically, magically bring romance into your life.

1. Adjust your thinking toward the positive, health-giving, and pleasurable aspects of romance. Nowadays there is little danger in adult romantic encounters; and as we have seen, there is no sin in romance even if it be consummated.

2. The trio or 'trine' of natures that attract romance are those associated with water: Pisces the Fish, Cancer the Crab, and Scorpio the Scorpion. Table VII-1 shows how this trine of natures automatically brings to you different types of romantic encounters.

Nature	Type of Romantic Encounter Desired
Fish	Spiritual
Crab	Home and Hearth
Scorpion	Lustful

Table VII-1

3. Assume the nature of the type you desire, either for a short period (Chapter I) or a long period (Chapter III). Romance will flow to you automatically.

Desire Driveth Us On but Quickly Fadeth

When the young sheik visiteth the city, he is often attracted by houses of joy. In those houses of joy he is lured by the beautiful women who pretend to be maidens. Similarly when thou journeyest across the desert of life the attractive oasis beckoneth unto thee. Thy desires, whether for refreshment from the well in the desert or from the maiden's offer, are equally demanding; however, when thou arrivest thou findest often that the well is muddy and the water unappetizing, for the oasis is overcrowded with others who have been attracted by its promise. Yet thou desirest water still. Often it is true that after a sip of the muddy water thou canst travel on to a plainer oasis where thou canst abide in a place less frequented, knowing then that here the water is pure.

Life would indeed be dull without attractive oases on the path. It would indeed be dull if thou didst not find and become acquainted with companions whose ways are different from thine own. But as I have told thee before, the law of attraction is stronger than that of complementarity. Assuredly thou must explore. Yet too often thou art trapped by those older than thee and yet not wiser, who claim that when thou hast once visited the attractive oasis thou must abide there for the rest of thy natural life. Also, thou must know that the binding I did discuss before will occur more strongly between man and woman if thou guardest not against it; for when thou sharest salt and warmth, and meldest thy body with that of a woman, thou becomest bonded unto her.

Gisela Unknowingly Traps Jacques

Student File 5G-2BA

Gisela M is an experienced older woman, a long-time student of the School and a dear friend of ours; she lives in Paris, France. After her unsuccessful marriage ended, she decided that life held more for her as a businesswoman than as a housewife. Gisela is attractive and has many romances, but sees no reason why she should tie herself down to anyone and give up her successful career.

Turmoil came into her life in the form of a 22-year-old student, Jacques. Gisela was probably flattered by this attractive youngster's attentions, and the affair had about it all the romantic euphoria that only the young seem able to bring to a love affair. Finally they became lovers. After a time, though, Jacques' possessiveness and intensity began to interfere with Gisela's independence. Also she found Jacques far less sophisticated than most of her friends. She tried to push him out of her life, and finally in a stormy scene she had him physically removed from her apartment by another of her friends. Late that night she received a call from the gendarmerie: They had fished a half-dead Jacques out of the Seine. Whether this was a suicide attempt or just a piece of manipulation we don't know; anyway, Gisela unhappily took him back into her life. She wrote to us in much distress wanting, as she put it, the reverse of a love spell: some magic whereby she could successfully get Jacques to leave without hurting him.

It turned out that Jacques was a Leo—one of the most loyal of all natures. Almost no matter what you say to a Leo; once he or she has become your friend, he will remain loyal. If he finds out that a friend is really being underhanded with him, it temporarily shatters his world. Consequently we warned Gisela that she would have to deal very delicately with Jacques and not try to thrust him out of her life as she had before. We advised her first to find another companion for Jacques, one whom he could learn to trust; and then to follow the path we gave her to unbind the ties between them. Sexual ties can be very deep, especially when it is the first intense experience for one of the partners. Gisela was able slowly and carefully to wean Jacques of his romantic love for her; and they still remain friends. Yet to do this, she had to use all her skill and sophistication, and for many months her life remained a turmoil. She lost several good business contacts, just because she let Jacques become bonded to her.

Astromantically Avoiding the Spell of Desire

Desire strikes in the most surprising places. People who are altogether unsuited for one another often find themselves in the throes of a passionate love affair because of the attraction they feel for each other. This attraction may derive from past lifetimes lived together or from a likeness of natures or, as Ibn Saud noted, from a total difference between natures. In this case, each finds novelty and excitement in exploring the other's ideas and habits. The problem is: Most people are unable to separate in their own minds honest desire from the qualities and natures that when combined would make a lasting, long-term relationship work. Desire often runs its course quickly; however, if the relationship is consummated the couple are bound together for they have shared many things, just as in a friendship ritual. Perhaps they have bathed together; they have eaten together or perhaps they have even, in the simile of the romantic magazines, 'used one another's toothbrush.' Any of these sharings can bind them together. Anthropologists have also noticed that the sexual act tends to bind the male to the female; for Mother Nature arranges it so that the natural result of such sex acts, the child, is to be protected and consequently the male instinct leads one who has committed the act of fathering to wait around for the birth. If you enter into any relationship that is based purely on desire, and the partners have little in common, you must be careful not to bind yourself to the partner, and equally careful to try your best not to let him get bound to you. One way of doing this is to wear closed rings on your fingers. These will diminish your susceptibility to psychic entanglement. Be honest with your partner about your needs, and be honest about your long-range expectations; your problems will be minimized.

When binding occurs as it did in Jacques' case, you have to act in such a way that the bond will be broken with minimum pain.

Using Your Incompatibility Wheel to Break Up a Relationship Painlessly

No matter how carefully you enter into a romance, you will occasionally get trapped. Additionally, you must not overlook the possibility of being ensnared by a magical procedure. On other occasions you may wish to break up the relationship between two other people who you can see are heading for disaster.

Just as you have learned how to attract friends and romance into your life by assuming the correct nature and looking for compatibilities, so you can also arrange for rejection by using the nature which most clashes with the person you want to reject, or by suggesting to one party of a relationship that he or she should behave more in the manner of an incompatible nature. To find the nature which is incompatible to yours, construct the Astromancy Incompatibility Computer shown in Figure VII-1. When you place point A over the sign of the person to be rejected, the arrows indicate the natures that are incompatible. All you have to do is assume one of these two natures, and the person will automatically—slowly and surely—depart from your life.

Do Not Let Thine Energies Be Consumed by Passion

In my day it was the custom for parents to arrange many marriages; and I say unto thee truly that most of these marriages endured far longer and were happier than those which the children of today arrange for themselves. When two people are brought together cold and a small fire is kindled, throughout their lives they use the energies that we are given to sustain the fire of their affection. When two people come together with great passionate desire, they use these energies to build a flaming pyre—and too often when the pyre is consumed ashes of hate are left. Like the good brickmaker, thou must build a slow fire that will last until thy death. To do this, the spark must be kindled first with casual acquaintanceship, then with friendship, and only then must all the tinder be ignited with the slow passion of long-lasting love. Thou mayest say, and I will not argue overly with thee, that arranged marriages had about them some unhappiness; but thou givest the parents no credit. Parents in my day did not punish their children by forcing them into unsuitable relationships. They knew who their children's friends were, and usually chose a marriage partner from among them. Only when it was a matter of great import to the State were marriages arranged outside our sheikdom.

Do not be driven off a cliff by thy passion and desire. Find instead the path to the plain that will lead thee surely to a safe haven in thine old age. Remember always that it is thy spirit which crieth out to another spirit for succor and companionship. Try if thou canst to ignore the whining demands of thy body and the superficial beauty of the dancing girl; for that superficial beauty will surely fade and die.

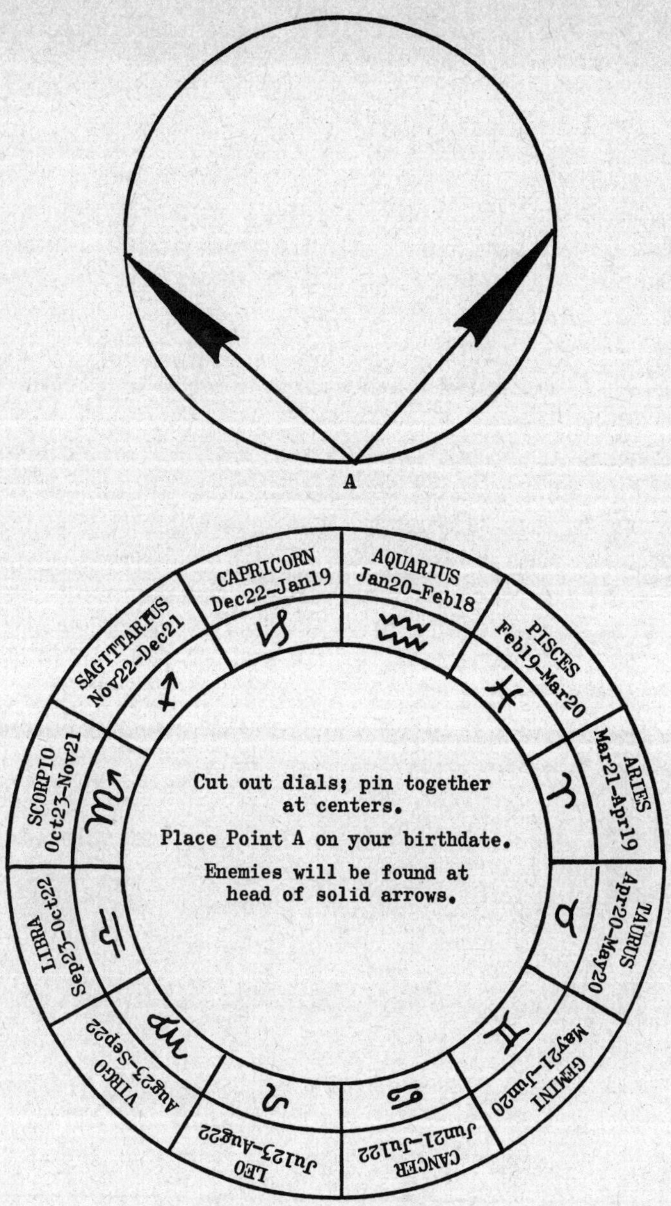

Figure VII-1
Your Astromantic Incompatibility Computer

Lonely Virgo Lily Becomes Much-Wooed Pisces Gina

Student File 3G-0BI

Lily R is a student in Miami, Florida. She is somewhat unique in being a native Floridian. In a way typical of the Virgo nature, she was born, grew up, and still lives in the same area of the state. Even when she went to college she did not stay on campus, but commuted each day from her home. When her brother moved away and her parents finally passed on, Lily found herself in her early thirties and totally alone. She knew many of the older people who lived in the area, but she had no friends at all of her own age. In her loneliness she wrote to us, not only wishing to take the course but also seeking friends. We had not had as much experience with people in those early days of our School and its course, and perhaps we were a little less careful than we might have been with our advice to Lily. We told her to take on the attributes of a Pisces, to relax, to go with the flow, and to take romance where she found it. Within a few weeks of our offering that advice she wrote to say she was giving up the course because she was too busy with many new friends.

Several years later we met Lily in person at a convention. She told us that although the magic had worked for her and she had indeed gotten all the friends she wanted, it was still a time of great unhappiness in her life. Within a week of turning herself into a Pisces she had locked on emotionally to an Aquarius and had bound herself to him emotionally by consummating the affair one romantic evening. He had encouraged her in her Pisces guise to date his other friends, but her Virgo background was still too strong within her for her to follow such a course. She was locked on to a most unsuitable partner; and even though many other men romanced her, still she remained monogamously faithful to her Aquarius. Through no real fault of his own, he led her a merry dance and she was dreadfully unhappy. The denouement came when he left town without giving a forwarding address and she, pregnant at the time, tried to trace him. She lost her lover's trail and ended up having a miscarriage alone and friendless in New Orleans. She returned to her own home a forlorn shadow of her former self.

One of the more retiring men from the group who was also a Virgo came looking for her one day, inquiring after her health and wondering where she had been. Gradually this casual acquaintance became a good friend who helped her in many little ways. Eventually their friendship turned into love, and Lily is now living within a happy and enduring compatible marriage.

Reviewing Your Path to Romance

Lily's story is really one of magic that went wrong, partially through our failure to investigate the situation thoroughly enough. This is one of the reasons we have learned to be so careful in giving advice by letter; for more often than not, people withhold some of the information we need for a proper assessment of their case.

Having a romance, being made love to or making love, is great fun and we think it should be indulged in far more often than it is; however, it should not be the basis for a lifetime relationship. Too often people share only a bed. To find romance, first you must act like an air sign and gain a circle of acquaintances. From these acquaintances, with the aid of your Friendship Dial, you can select a handful of friends. Then, using the trine of love, you can start a romance with any of these friends you wish. At all times, realize in your mind the difference between desire and affection. Of course the attractive person down the street would be fun to make love to! If you can make this come true, do it and get it out of your system; no blame. But do not confuse this with a true romance and love affair, which must be based on mutual understanding and friendship.

You can temporarily change your elemental nature so that you can more easily gratify your desire; but these personality changes are not for ever and you will eventually slip back into your old inborn ways. If in an altered personality you become bonded to another person, however, that bonding will remain even when you change back into your own natural birth personality. It is equally true that you should not try to change the personality of the one of whom you are now enamored; nor if you force that personality into a new mold, it too will slip back into its natural personality after a little while, and only ashes will remain. The Pygmalion story wherein the professor makes an urchin into a lady and falls in love with her is all very well as a story, and it will work if the natures of the people are compatible; but if you try to change the nature of your partner, disaster will surely follow.

Today you may be in a relationship (or thinking about one) which may never succeed for there is in it the underlying flaw of incompatibility of natures. While you and your spouse are still young, divorce should not be looked upon as a tragedy; instead, it is the completion of one chapter of your life and the opportunity to start another, better, more interesting chapter suited to your current needs.

Breathe Life into Another

At intervals a miracle doth occur in the desert. A small amount of rain doth fall; then the desert which was brown becometh green, and beautiful flowers appear and grass doth grow. Thus doth love water the spirit of a lonely heart. A small romance, and the couple involved do bloom and appear beautiful, even if only in the eyes of each other. Whence cometh this beauty of the body? It cometh from the change in the spirit! It cometh not from new attire or from the pots and jars of the purveyor of cosmetics. It is internal beauty which shineth like a clear light from heaven. This teacheth us that when one spirit toucheth another these spirits together grow and, like blossoms opening in the desert, make the mundane body flower. Provided only that this blossom be allowed to grow under the mutual cherishing of the dual spirits, the future is assured. If the blossom faileth, it doth so because the spirits of the couple are not compatible. No one should be blamed for such a failure; for if the spirits do not meld, no matter that the bodies are young and harmonious; still they will never be truly one. Above all, the authorities in the land (whether they be religious or secular) should not with mighty oaths proclaim that once married, people are sentenced for life to unhappiness and its attendant ill health.

Eleanor and Lew Get Handfasted

In their youth Eleanor and Lew were both hell-raisers. They really had a ball in the farm community where they lived. Because their natures were obviously similar, they often collaborated in the high jinks that teenagers get up to. Lew, however, was always looking for the blond, petite, curvaceous girls when his thoughts turned to romance. He seemed to overlook Eleanor, who was rather large-boned and a tomboy type. She seemed not to be to his liking—or was simply in his blind spot. Whenever he sowed some wild oats and came back with what he thought was a broken heart, Eleanor was there to comfort him. Yes, of course she was upset; for in her way she loved Lew even then. Yet every time Lew went off on a new romance she encouraged him, feeling that if he could just get it out of his system he would be better for it and would grow to a greater understanding. Lew and Eleanor were the best possible friends, each sharing the other's troubles and joys—except of course that Eleanor never told Lew how she really felt about him.

One winter's day nearly thirty years ago, as Lew remembers it, he suddenly woke up to the fact that he loved Eleanor. This sudden overnight realization left him stunned; but even though it was snowing hard, he walked over to Eleanor's and told her right out, as was his way, how he felt. Theirs was a whirlwind courtship and marriage, for within a couple of weeks they were married by the county clerk. All their friends shook their heads and said it would never last, and their parents were aghast at the abrupt civil ceremony.

But Lew and Eleanor were happy and they bloomed together, for they were of one nature, and the scrapes they had been in together had already melded their spirits.

Many years after their mundane wedding, they came to us because they felt that even though they were good friends, still the spiritual part of their life was not sealed. Meeting them, seeing how they worked and reacted together, it was obvious that their spirits were truly melded though in their minds they were still separate. So we performed for them a Wiccan marriage, wherein the bodies are bound together in a manner which guarantees the spirits will unite. Shortly after this handfasting Lew and Eleanor went through a terrifying and destructive calamity, a calamity we cannot describe here for it is still being sorted out in the courts. Let it suffice to say that any other marriage would probably have failed if subjected to this kind of stress. Yet when all their friends seemed to abandon them, when prosperity and health ebbed away, still they found strength in each other and still they shone with inner beauty. Seeing this, their friends came back and are now supporting them in their unsolved problems.

Theirs is the type of marriage or long-term spiritual commitment that you really want.

Soul-Mating Yourself with Another

Once you have found someone with whom you can be completely compatible and friendly, someone with whom romance has turned into love, then it is time to consider going through the spiritual procedure necessary to meld your two spirits, or as it is fashionably called, 'soul mating.' First you should do the procedure for friendship from Chapter VI; then live together for a year and a day; and then proceed to the following steps.

From the Astromantic point of view, when a couple decide they are ready to meld spiritually, their decision means that two separate beings are going to form a new mutually supportive being; and the life of this being starts at some definite point in time. We usually recommend that this point in time be selected as a time of Leo; for Leo is the most loyal of all the signs. Review now the section in Chapter III on being reborn. Calculate a time when Leo energy will be available to you, preferably on a day of the new moon; for you wish this loyalty and mutual regard to grow as the moon grows.

Make sure you have enough space in your artificial womb for two people to lie in fetal position. Each individual should crawl into the artificial womb at the time of his own sign. If you are both of the same sign, you should enter at the same time. If one is already a Leo, he should spend 24 hours in the artificial womb. The key thing here is that you both emerge together, preferably embracing as you re-enter the world.

You are now soul-mated.

To make a more perfect match, if you wish you can consult an astrologer and find out from him what is the best possible day and time for your new beginning; then at that day and time you can get a Witch group to perform a handfasting for you so that you are sure your spirits will be melded at the most auspicious time.

Putting the Knowledge of This Chapter to Work in Your Life

Romantic needs should not be confused in your life with a long-term commitment to one other person. That commitment will come in due time; and when it does it will be truly wonderful for you.

To gain romance:

- Use the trine of love to bring romance into your life.

To avoid entanglements:

- Wear closed rings at all encounters and be honest with your partner that this is not a long-term love relationship.

To break off a relationship:

- Use the nature indicated on the Astromantic Incompatibility Computer.

To become a soul-mate:

- Check that the person in question is really totally compatible with your birth nature.
- Be reborn together.

Chapter Eight

LET ASTROMANCY PROTECT YOU

What This Chapter Can Do for You

The quadra of your nature enables you to protect yourself and your possessions from both psychic and physical attacks. Using the knowledge of the quadras, you can protect yourself and your property against:

- Evil Eye
- Psychic Attack
- Door-to-Door Sales
- Telephone Solicitations and Threats
- Personal Violence
- Thieves

The Quality of Thy Nature

The energy that cometh to thee and formeth thy nature is not only of an elemental form; but it doth also possess a quality. Water, as thou dost know, can be smooth or turbulent; or it can become as fixed as ice. The earth can be as light as dust, as resilient as clay, or as solid as the rocks of Mount Ararat. Similarly, fire can be controlled to warm thy food; or it can be as all-consuming as the fire that doth burn whole towns and destroy the heather of the mountainside. Sometimes it cometh unto us in a fixed form, as when lava doth flow from a volcano. Indeed fire in this form is so fixed that in the past many did worship it and call it Jehovah.[1] *Air too can be a warm gentle zephyr—or a hot destructive shamal.*[2] *Thus it is not only that thou behavest like an element, but thou hast also a quality; for the energies that come from beyond space to the earth have both elemental and qualitative natures. Each of these qualities owneth its place in the scheme that Allah hath decreed in His wisdom; for is it not true that the dress of fine silk is just as useful in its time as is a coarse linen cloak which doth fend off the whims of weather? Yea, verily, it is true that the linen doth stand up to wear somewhat better than the silk; however, the silk doth show the authority of leadership, and the woman wearing silk rarely hath cause to work in such a way that her garment suffereth damage. The quality that is put on by the person wearing different clothes is the same quality that thou canst use to defend thyself in time of threat. As I have told thee, thou canst for short periods of time change thy nature and in this way gain all that thou dost desire and deserve. However, when thou wishest to protect thyself thou shouldst do it for many turns of the Wheel of Heaven, not just for this day. Thus thou shouldst not change thine innermost nature and quality to protect thyself, but shouldst instead use and rein-*

---

[1] Arnold Toynbee "Crucible of Christianity"

[2] Strong storm wind of the desert

force the strengths that thou hast by thy nature in order to make thy citadel secure against all comers.

Millionaire Alvin Fails to Get His Way

Student File 3Y-4LC

Alvin G is a multi-millionaire living in Dallas, Texas. He became interested in Witchcraft when his first wife died and he was haunting the singles bars looking for a new liaison. Alvin's interest in most things, with the one exception of money, was totally superficial; so he touched only lightly on the precepts of the religion and never really modified the deeper areas of his life. However, he really wanted to become an initiated Witch so he could attend some of the inner circle meetings which are run by various groups around the nation. Getting to be initiated became almost an obsession with him. He assumed that, just as he had with other clubs and societies, he should be able to buy his way in and buy his initiation. It was just a matter of negotiating the price. With a view to this, he bought the local group a small farm, and paid to build a meeting hall on the land. The group was extremely grateful, of course, and several of its members approached the Scorpio high priestess, Daisy H, to suggest that Alvin should be initiated. The group feared that if Alvin was denied initiation he would figure some way to take back his most generous gifts.

Daisy decided she should do what is called a mirror ritual so that Alvin would tend to forget and to overlook the Wiccan group, the farm, and the meeting place. She did this because she felt a mirror ritual was the most appropriate for her nature. It did not seem to work, however; for Alvin was more than ever insistent on his qualifications and his right to initiation. At this point Daisy wrote to us, telling us what she had done and asking what her next step should be. We pointed out to her that she had done a personal ritual for defense; whereas what she should have done was a ritual for the group and for the land and the building.

It turned out that the time of signature on the deed and the time of the group's formation both had Arian aggressive attack qualities and thus instead of doing a mirror ritual she should have put up a defensive thorn thicket around the group and the property. We told her that if she erected this psychic defensive thicket properly, Alvin would either settle down and study to qualify for a genuine initiation; or, seeing the psychic thicket, would stop bothering them. After the ritual was completed, Alvin lost interest in the group and so was not initiated at that time. Recently, however, we hear that he has undergone severe finaicial setbacks. Rumor is that since the loss of his money, he is beginning to study the Craft seriously again and should be initiated before you read this book.

Using Your Quadra to Defend Yourself

As Ibn Saud pointed out, cosmic energies from beyond space have not only different elemental natures but also qualities. Table VIII-1 shows these qualities. The left-hand column shows the elemental character of each of the heavenly areas. You can see from the Table that the twelve natures of the Wheel divide into four horizontal Trines and three vertical Quadras. In Chapter VII we used the Trine of Love and Romance, and in Chapter VI we used the Trine of Friendship. In following chapters we will show you how the other Trines can be utilized.

In this chapter we are interested in the vertical columns or Quadras. Sometimes you will hear astrologers talking of 'cardinal,' 'fixed,' and 'mutable' signs. These are the same Quadras under different names.

When you wish to defend yourself or your property against any threat, you must fit your defense to the basic quality with which you or your property is imbued. Since you know your birth nature, you need merely read to the top of the Table to find out what your quality is and the bottom to

	Cardinal	Fixed	Mutable	
Earth	♑	♉	♍	Trine of Wealth (Chapter X)
Fire	♈	♌	♐	Trine of Dominance and Control (Chapter IX)
Water	♋	♏	♓	Trine of Love (Chapter VII)
Air	♎	♒	♊	Trine of Friendship (Chapter VI)
	Quadra of Attack	Quadra of the Mirror	Quadra of Invisibility	

Table VIII-1
Quadras and Trines of Your Nature

learn in which quadra you fall. Other items are only slightly more difficult. The quality of a marriage is judged from the time, date, and place at which it was consummated; a group by the time, date, and place it was formed. The time of a building or other material possession is usually determined by the time, date, and place at which it came into your physical possession. Thus Daisy was a fixed water sign; however, the coven and the building turned out to have a cardinal quadra-of-attack quality, so protection for the building and the coven had to be done in a manner appropriate to an attack-quadra sign.

Three types of protection are used in Astromancy:

1. Attacks of the aggressor—The aggressor is one who finds that for him attack is the best form of defense.
2. Mirror—Being fixed by nature, this person erects a defensive mirror around himself, thus reflecting back any attack onto the aggressor.
3. Invisibility—One of mutable nature blends with his background and disappears into the crowd, camouflaging or concealing himself.

Table VIII-2 shows the three defensive methods appropriate to the various birth natures and their respective qualities. In the past you may have tried various protective devices, only to find they did not work for you though they had been shown to work adequately for other people. This is because the defensive method you were using was not appropriate to the quality of your nature.

Quality of Nature	Defensive Method
Cardinal	Attack
Fixed	Mirror
Mutable	Invisibility

Table VIII-2
Quality of Nature and Defensive Methods

Protective Methods for the Quadra of Attack

The quality of the natures in the Quadra of Attack is such that they are strong and determined, good leaders, and quick to respond to any slight by attacking the aggressor. Thus to defend against any attack, the attacked person or property should be made to look extremely aggressive. A person should simulate anger; a vehicle should be painted in an aggressive color (probably red); and all objects should be clearly labeled, "The property of ____________." If a person having this quality receives a bill through the mail which is not due, that bill should be returned with a very aggressive letter to the manager of the company involved. A person being harassed on the phone should respond with violence to the caller, topping each epithet used with a more belligerent one. When faced with these ploys, most attackers retreat. Houses belonging to Quadra-of-Attack people should be protected by notices of electronic equipment on the premises and by "Beware of the Dog" (or some other animal) signs. For psychic protection, a triple circle of salt and sulphur should be laid down in daylight around the property where everyone can see it. When all else fails, a protective ritual should be done at high noon on the day of a new moon. A typical ritual would be as follows:

'GET THEE GONE' Ritual

> At high noon on the day of a new moon, take two red candles and a photograph of the person to be kept away. Light the candles and look into their flames, thinking strongly of the person being defeated. Burn the picture, saving the ashes. Take one candle (still burning) in each hand and smash their flaming ends violently together, while you yell at the top of your voice,
>
> "____________ (name), get thee gone!"
>
> Divide the ash into three portions; divide the candle drip-

pings into three portions. Mail one portion of ash and one portion of drippings to the attacker. After nine days mail a second portion of each to the attacker. After another nine days, mail the final portions to the attacker. He will leave you alone.

Florella Stops the Robbers

Student File 2G-6WZ

Florella W is a student from Harlem. She originally wrote to us for a protective ritual for her property because she was constantly being ripped off. She lived in a neighborhood where a high incidence of theft is chronic. After studying Florella's situation, we decided that her apartment was in the Quadra of Attack. We told her to paint the door red and nail to it two crossed bones. Additionally we suggested she place a small sign near the doorknob saying, "When opening door, please do not let the snakes escape as the cold will harm them." Since the day she changed her door, Florella has never lost so much as a penny, even though she lives (as we said) in an area with a high crime rate.

Protective Methods for Quadra-of-the-Mirror Natures

The quality of Mirror-Quadra natures is fixed, so that people having this quality wish to remain in one fixed place and do not wish to be moved, no matter that type of attack is launched against them. The only way to defend this nature adequately is to surround it with a mirror so that any attack is reflected back against the attacker. If your nature is that of the Mirror Quadra, you should use the new plastic reflective coating preparations on the windows of your home and your car. Wear mirror sunglasses. If someone calls and annoys you on the phone, repeat back to him the words he uses. For psychic attack, on the night of a full moon place horseshoes around your home with their points outward. A good ritual to do is:

PROTECTIVE MIRROR Ritual

Since time immemorial polished surfaces, especially of bronze and steel, have been used with appropriate charming to reflect back the harmful intent of ill-wishers and casters of the evil eye. A mirror by itself is inert and neutral; so to make it work for you, place a picture of yourself behind the mirror as shown in Figure VIII-1. Then use a ritual to activate the combination.

> Light four orange candles. Hold the mirror flat against your heart. Stand facing north and chant,
>
> "Mirror, Mirror, work for me.
> From slings and arrows keep me free.
> As I will, so mote it be."
>
> Repeat the chant while you face east, then south, then west. Repeat it again while you hold the mirror face down at floor level; and again while you hold it face up at arm's length above your head. (This means you will say the chant a total of six times.) Let the candles burn out in their own time.
>
> Reinforce this protective ritual once every five days until the danger is past. If you can place the mirror with

Figure VIII-1
Your Mirror of Protection
(Picture is entirely hidden behind mirror)

your picture behind it where the attacker can see it, this is the best possible defense. If such an arrangement cannot be made, you should bury the mirror face up in dry sand to which you have added a little sulphur and salt.

George Rids His Life of Bad Influences

Student File 5Y-6US

George Q lives in Scottsdale, Arizona, and was part of the retirement community there. He was no mean occultist; however, he was always getting himself into trouble by being too obliging to his friends. This is an Aquarian habit: Aquarians fear loneliness, and in order to keep their friends they tend to do such things as become co-signers on notes. Inevitably some of these notes cause problems, and George seemed always to be plagued by bill collectors and telephone solicitations. He had his telephone number changed; still they tracked him down. He even had it unlisted; still they seemed to be able to get it. He met us at a psychic seminar in Phoenix. We told him his trouble was that people would remember him because he was so friendly, and that he needed to do a mirror ritual to reflect back the attacks. George did the ritual and additionally invented a new name which reversed the order of the letters in his actual name. It is not illegal in the United States to use a pseudonym. When he put his telephone in this name, no one could find him; and when he told people his name, very few remembered it. Thus he easily overcame his problems.

Protective Methods for Those of the Quadra of Invisibility

A basic law of physics is that energy has to be stopped if it is to cause damage. It is the absorption of radiation energy, for instance, that kills. If the energy passed through without being stopped, those in its path would not be harmed. The same is true of psychic energy. If you become psychically invisible, you will never be harmed by energies directed at you.

In order to defend yourself or your property, therefore, if you are in the Quadra of Invisibility, you must become invisible. If your house is in a city, make it identical to all its neighbors. Paint it in precisely the same colors, and make the front yard precisely match those on either side of it. If you are in the country, you should screen your dwelling with bushes and trees, and perhaps paint it with camouflage colors. When you are in a crowd of people your attire must exactly match theirs. When you are at a party, you must not in any way be distinguishable from others at that party. You must match not only your attire but also your actions and voice to those around you. You may have a tendency to dress in pastel colors and to be very wishy-washy. You must overcome this habit if you are to avoid attack, for in a brightly colored crowd your pastels make you different and thus noticeable.

If your telephone is a problem, in your case you should list it in among the Smiths or the Wilsons; and when someone annoys you he should be answered with absolute silence. Bill collectors who come to you in error should also be met with a blank stare. If you are verbally attacked, put on the look of the idiot. Let it all flow by you as if you were not even there. If you are attacked psychically, again you should completely ignore it. After one experience of this, you should be able to get your mind in such a state that you don't even notice a psychic attack. Your total defense is to ignore any attack, making absolutely no response to it. To aid in this, an invisibility ritual is often useful.

INVISIBILITY Ritual

(Best performed at twilight on day of new moon)

Bathe quietly and gently. Put on a clean loose-fitting garment and go to some place where no one will see you. Light a small white candle. Around yourself and the candle, cast an imaginary circle by pointing your finger at the ground. Rotate upon your axis (that is, pirouette in place) saying quietly,

> "I am surrounded by the pure white light of the Gods.
> All that is good shall stay with me.
> All that is evil shall go on its way and cause me no harm."

Quietly blow out the candle, saying,

> "As I will, so mote it be."

It is best either to burn or to bury the remains of the candle, or place it among other used candles in a drawer.

Dolores Drives the Sorcerer Berserk

Student File 2G-8XR

Dolores G, a Pisces by nature, lived in Mexico City. When she was young, she somehow incurred the wrath of a Spanish sorcerer or 'brujo.' He swore a mighty oath that he would be avenged and would cause her never to marry. Dolores was a young child when this happened, and had quite forgotten the sorcerer's curse by the time she started dating. She fell in love with a young Spanish nobleman, Juan-Carlos, who was visiting Mexico for the first time. Perhaps through jealousy, one of Dolores' friends told Juan-Carlos of the curse. He immediately went to another brujo and got all the protective amulets he could obtain for Dolores; but they did no good. For as the wedding day approached Dolores seemed to be more and more on edge and arguments between the lovers multiplied. Things reached such a state that the wedding was postponed.

At this time Dolores, who had earlier been a student of the School, wrote to us about her problem. We told her to get rid of all the amulets and to do the invisibility ritual given above. We traveled astrally to see Dolores a couple of times after she did the ritual, and could see negative thoughtforms (apparently from the brujo) going right through her. Soon, despite the brujo's efforts, the marriage was performed and Dolores now lives in Madrid with her new husband.

Under normal circumstances, one might say that the removal of the amulets which Juan-Carlos had bought for Dolores meant that she was no longer reminded of the curse, and that the curse which was all in her mind was therefore inoperative. But we can assure you that energies from the curse were present around Dolores even on her wedding day. They did not affect her because she was able totally to ignore them.

Later we heard that the brujo had worked hard at his curse; that in fact he worked himself into a severe illness. In his attempts to stop the wedding, he went to the Basilica of Guadalupe and tried to direct negative energy at Dolores actually as she knelt at the altar. He expended his energy in vain; for she was perfectly immune to his attacks, and they passed through her just as light passes through clear glass.

Balancing Thy Wheel of Life

The wheel which is not round traveleth unevenly along the path of life; and if it be too far out of round, it becometh useless and breaketh on the first small obstruction lying along the caravan route. By the laws of the universe, the energies from the Wheel of Heaven that thou seest above thy head are balanced one against another. The forces which act on thee are in perfect harmony; and thus it must be with thy life. As thou proceedest along thy path, thou must proceed in balance. If thou art overbalanced toward any one element, thou wilt make rough that which is smooth and wilt be unable to surmount any roughness in the path. Thou must imitate the action of a spinning top. If thou placest weights at equal spaces around the rim of a top, the child can still spin it in perfect balance and harmony. But if thou placest one weight on the rim of the top, it will not spin. As it is with the top, so should it be with thy life.

How Claire Became a Great Trial Lawyer

Student File 3G-3AD

Claire N now lives in a large midwestern city.[3] She joined our School when she felt that her whole life was going to pieces. Claire had been a brilliant law student, graduating very close to the top of her class. On the strength of her grade average she had been able to obtain an excellent position with one of the city's larger law firms.

Claire's father had died when she was still in her teens, but her mother had invested the insurance money wisely and had been able both to support herself and to help Claire through college, even though this meant she had to get a temporary job with the postal service and Claire herself had to get some substantial student loans.

Now, with her position secure, Claire was able to repay her mother some of the money paid toward her education; and her mother was able to give up her job. Very soon, though, Claire found that working in a law office was not quite the same thing as being the star of her class, although she got a good salary and could see that in a few years' time she would have her opportunity to shine in the courtroom. The drudgery of searching for appropriate precedents, the file work, and the research work were assigned to Claire while the firm's more senior members participated in the drama of the courtroom. Claire saw the results of her own research only in the newspapers, when the trial lawyer won or lost a prominent case on which she had worked.

At this time her mother's health broke down and she had a major heart attack. Claire therefore gritted her teeth and carried on with her humdrum work, suppressing her fiery nature. Slowly she fell ill of what the doctors could only call 'non-specific ailments,' meaning that they didn't really know

---

[3]Because she is so well known, we cannot give you even the name of the town.

what was wrong with her. Her work grew more and more superficial; and when she was reproached for this, she grew angry and defended herself by attacking. Eventually the law firm told her in no uncertain terms that she had better shape up or prepare to ship out.

Claire began to worry that she was hexed, and wrote to us as old friends who might be able to help her. Our advice was essentially to balance her nature by finding a position where she could use her fiery attack characteristics to their full advantage. She took our advice and became the public defender for a small town near the city in which she lived. In this role she was quite brilliant, and immediately regained her health and her pleasant personality. Because she now had to do research work for her own cases, she could comprehend how important that aspect of the work was; for if in this position she didn't do it suitably, she could see the results in her cases right away. In this manner, her life got into a more balanced condition.

Soon she gained a reputation as an attorney who could win the most difficult and complex cases for her clients. Within six months of becoming a public defender, she was offered a chance to be the assistant trial lawyer in a major murder case. When the leading attorney fell ill, she took over and stunningly convinced the jury that her client was not guilty. Of course this success led to other opportunities to show her abilities. In all her trial work, though, she still balances her nature by doing her own research.

Because Claire learned the value of being able to channel her fiery energy into other natural characteristics, she was able to achieve a smooth balanced approach to life and hence to her cases.

The Wheel Balancing Disk of Your Life

To achieve balance in your life, you must occasionally take on the natures of the other elements of your own quadra, though we do not recommend that you try for ever to change the underlying quality of your nature. We did not, for instance, recommend to Claire that she change from an attack quadra to a mutable hiding quadra. We suggested instead that she achieve in her life a good balance rather than continually suppressing her fire elemental nature. The easiest way to get this balance is to use the three zodiacal amulets as we told you in Chapter I to bring in the missing energies. Claire was not hexed; she was psychically unbalanced.

Another way of balancing your life is to make a personal disk. To do this, look at Table VIII-1, to find your own natal sign and quadra. In order to achieve balance, you must bring in elements from the other natal signs of your quadra. To use Claire's case as an example: She was an Aries, the second sign down in the left-hand column. To achieve a balance, she had to bring into her life elements of earth (Capricorn), water (Cancer), and air (Libra). We had her make a disk as shown in Figure VIII-2, with four quarters. Around its edge she inscribed her own sign and the three other signs, as shown in the figure. Figures VIII-3 and VIII-4 show balancing disks for the other quadras. Copy the disk appropriate to yourself onto heavy paper and color its segments. When you are having trouble in your life, place the center of your disk very carefully on the tip of a ball-point pen (Fig. VIII-5). Look down on it and think "Balance!" while you spin it with your finger. You must learn to do this delicate procedure even when you are under stress; for it is in looking down on the disk and being able to keep it in balance that you will be able automatically to achieve the balance that will overcome many of life's problems for you.

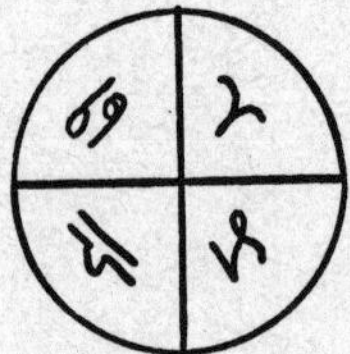

Figure VIII-2
Disk for Quadra of Attack

Figure VIII-3
Disk for Quadra of the Mirror

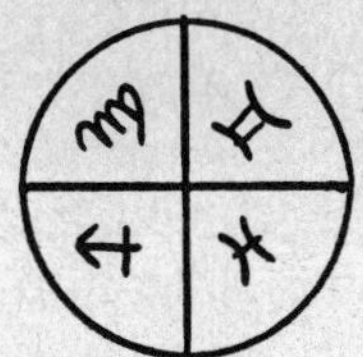

Figure VIII-4
Disk for Quadra of Invisibility

Figure VIII-5
Spinning a Quadra for Balance

Using the Teachings of This Chapter

If you are under attack, the first thing you need to do is look up your nature in Table VIII-1 and decide which defensive method is most appropriate to the quality of your nature. If you are of an attack quadra, attack those who are troubling you. Be bold and fearsome. Simulate a little violence if necessary. Make great use of red colors and bulky, overpowering jewelry and accessories.

If you are of the mirror quadra, you do not wish to move to the attack but remain exactly in the position where you find yourself. Take a fixed position with attackers, never varying your front; and when necessary, use mirror techniques to show the attackers how foolish they really are.

If you are of the invisibility quadra you should disappear into the crowd and psychically become as clear as pure glass so that the attacks pass right through you and you do not at any time even acknowledge their existence.

Lastly, throughout your life you should achieve a balanced nature; for when your nature is balanced, attacks that could occur through the other elements will automatically be warded off; and trouble that you might get yourself into by overemphasizing your own elemental nature will be avoided.

Chapter Nine

ASTROMANTICALLY GUIDING AND DOMINATING OTHER MORTALS

What This Chapter Will Do for You

Getting into a supervisory role or a role of leadership can be a most important early step on your pathway to success. This chapter will teach you how to use a Mastery Circle and to combine it with the Trine of Dominance to

- Influence others to your way
- Get decisions made in your favor
- Revise unfavorable opinions and decisions
- Direct others even when they are not in your presence

The Mastery Nature above Thee and the Subservient Nature below Thee

In my youth there was a game much played which today is called 'Scissors, Stone, Paper.' Each player doth on a given signal indicate with his hand whether he be scissors, stone, or paper. The stone doth blunt the scissors; the paper doth wrap the stone; and the scissor doth cut the paper. Thus these three devices form a circle[1] *in which none is altogether superior over the other for each hath its strengths but each can be overcome by one of the others. When Allah in His great generosity arranged the heavens so that energies from them would give mortal men differing natures, in His wisdom He also arranged that each succeeding sign should have dominance in its way over the one that preceded it. Thus fire can heat and vanquish water; water by its nature maketh heavy the light air signs; the wind can blow the sands of the desert or even wear down the mountains and overcome them; and fire must always submit to and be smothered by earth. In the wisdom of Allah the Wheel of the Heavens is perfectly balanced, for each succeeding sign can dominate the one before it and yet in its turn is dominated by the one that followeth it.*

Steve Enjoys Innumerable Conquests

Student File 2Y-8AR

When he came to us Steve was already a practicing occultist. He was fascinated by his power over other people, especially over women. He had used this power to taste all the fruits of life and he was worried to see how easily people could be swayed. After we got to know him a little, we found that this power concerned him so much he had at times even contemplated suicide; for he did not trust himself to use it wisely. In fact, as he told us later, he had used it to gratify his

---

[1]Shown in Figure IX-1

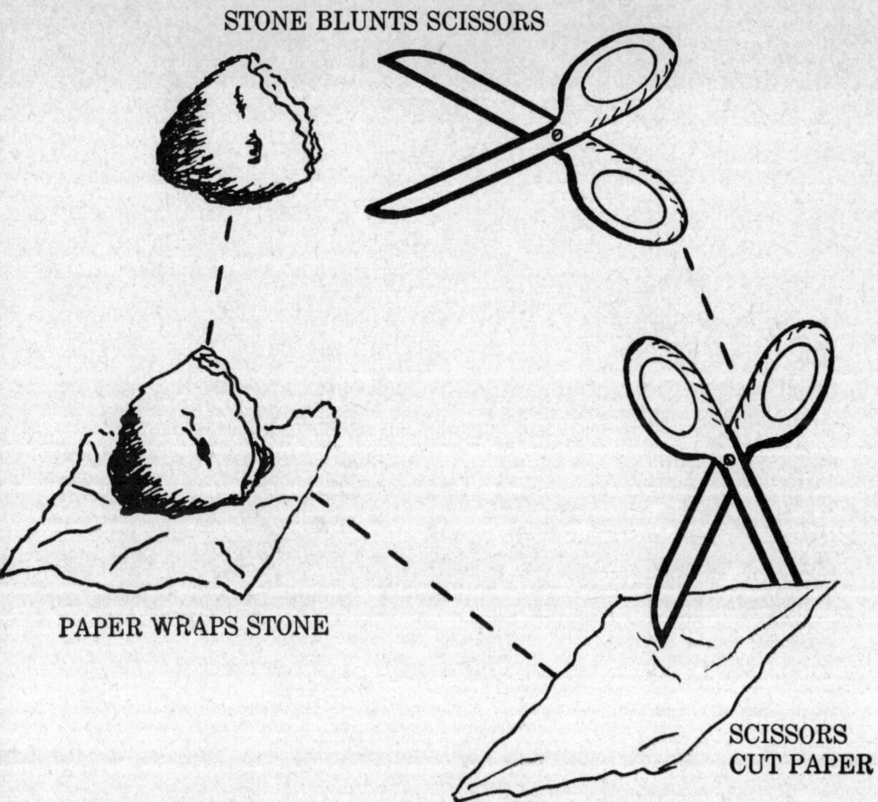

Figure IX-1
Strength and Weakness Circle of Domination

least whim and had become somewhat debauched and sated. Anything he wanted, he could get almost instantly.

He had come upon the method he used quite by accident, apparently; but his method has a sound basis in Astromantic fact. When Steve wished to dominate a person or to obtain a thing, he would find the birthdate of the person or object he wanted, and then he would assume the characteristics of the sign that mastered it. By doing this he could always attain his objective, no matter whether it was a lady's love, a loan from a bank, or a new car. It had never failed him. Because the path of life was so easy for him, he held life itself in low esteem. Only when he understood that the use of magic to attain every object robs life in this world of its spice and its value as a method of teaching the spirit, did he finally give up the use of magic and instead use his natural abilities to achieve his goals.

Your Circle of Mastery

As Ibn Saud taught and as Steve's experience confirmed to us, each sign has another sign which is subservient to it. The wheel of signs in Figure IX-2 shows this natural sequence of subservience. As you read around the circle in a clockwise direction, each nature has in itself something that can overcome the previous nature. If you wish to get your way with an Aries, for instance, you should assume the earth characteristics of a Taurus so that you can overcome the Arian fire with the smothering effect of earth. If you wish to overcome a Taurus, the air nature Gemini with its quickness of thought will soon confuse and wear away the resistance of a solid Taurus. The air nature Gemini in its turn can be mastered by the water nature Cancer, whose flowing presence and changes of direction will make the light and breezy Gemini heavy. Similarly, Cancer can be mastered by the fire of a Leo; for the heat of the fire will make the water evaporate. To use the Circle of Mastery, all you have to do is select the sign one around in a clockwise direction from the one you wish to master.

Typical Examples of the Use of Mastery

- Getting a bank loan

1. Go in and discuss the possibility of a loan with the bank officer. Do not ask for the loan at that time; instead, either get the birthdate of the loan officer or form your own opinion as to the date.

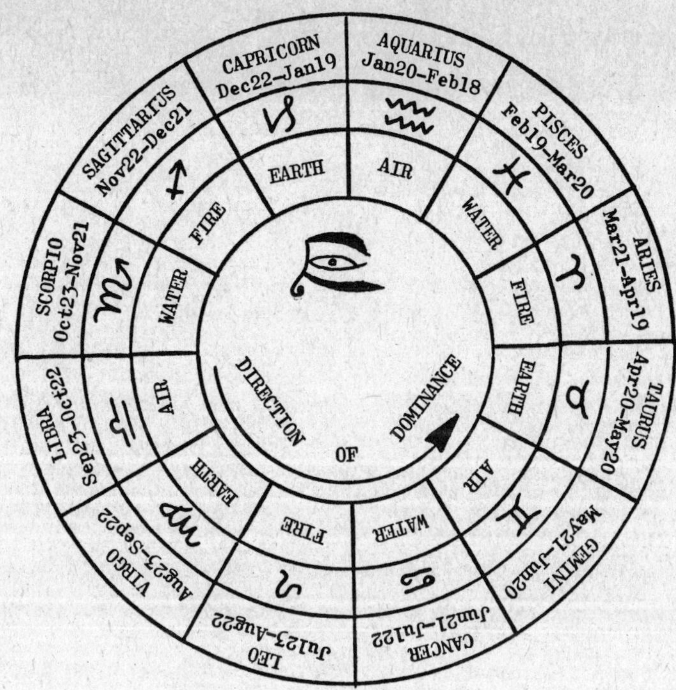

Figure IX-2
Your Wheel of Dominance

2. Assume the nature of a sign that masters the bank officer's nature (Chapter I) and if possible, set up your interview in the time of that nature (Chapter III).

3. Complete all the paperwork and detailed work you can ahead of time; then go in and get the loan.

- Filing a complaint or returning merchandise

1. Get an interview with the supervisor of the salesperson who is causing you the problem. This may be a single interview, so first ascertain the nature of the supervisor.

2. Excuse yourself for a moment and put on the appropriate amulet so that you can get energy to dominate the situation.

- Getting Rid of Unwanted People

1. In this case you probably know the nature of the person to be removed from your path.

2. Make a long-term adjustment in your nature (Chapter III) so that you can bring influence to bear for several days.

You will find that the natures you assume will work not only in face-to-face situations but also on the minds of people you have met long after you have left their immediate presence.

Every Herd Needeth Its Leader

In the far distant past when Homo Sapiens came unto this small planet from who knoweth where, even in those ancient days and even in the small groups in which they came, still each group had its leader. Without their leaders they would have been as the sands of the desert, blown without plan or pattern in all directions. Look thou around thee. See the mighty works of man. Without leadership they would all fall in anarchy and disarray. Even if thou likest not thy present leaders, still the very fact that the leader is active giveth thee something to rail against; and by thy noise thou makest other leaders take up thy cause. If thou dost watch any group of animals that have the slightest degree of social intercourse, thou wilt observe that among them there are competent leaders who keep danger at bay. By the strength thou canst gain from my poor words and the energies of the Wheel of Heaven, thou too wilt rise above thy fellow man, and people will look to thee for leadership. I say unto thee: It is thine for the taking. Assuredly thou wilt make an occasional error; but which leader doth not err? Canst thou not act more wisely than those whom thou daily seest reviled? In the great Wheel of the Heavens we have the fiery sun that doth lead us into each succeeding day, and it is in this nature and its trine companions that thou wilt find thy leadership powers.

Quiet Elouise Raises $180,000

Student File 3G-5WX

Elouise B is the wife of a small-town Georgia politician. She is a typical southern lady; and we often suspect that such ladies are the actual driving force behind the successes of their men. Elouise, however, had drifted with the southern culture and had become a passive bystander at her husband's campaigns. In the 1970's Georgia politics became very complex and difficult with the entry of such people as Jimmy Carter into the previously settled and quiet arena; in that arena the last real activity had been the civil-rights movement of the early 1960's. Thus Elouise's husband Clay was faced with a strenuous uphill battle in his fight for re-election.

With the women's lib movement coming along, one of Clay's aides conceived the idea that Elouise should be brought more to the front; his suggestion received support when Clay's party saw the publicity that Rosalynn and Miss Lillian achieved for Governor, then President, Carter. Time had hung heavy on Elouise's hands, and she had been taking our course. Now she did all she could to avoid getting involved in Clay's campaign short of appearing actually opposed to his candidacy. When opinion polls showed that Clay was losing, it was decided that Elouise should head up the local multiple-sclerosis fund drive. This meant she would have to go out and speak for the drive, and solicit funds for it on her own. She asked that, because this was such a deserving cause, we at the School do a money ritual to help her get the money quickly and let her get back to her quiet studies.

When we reviewed the situation, we could see that getting the money quickly would not serve the purpose of gaining sufficient publicity to get Clay re-elected. The goal set for the fund drive was a mere $40,000, which was some 20 percent over the previous year's total, but Elouise was completely distraught at the thought of having to raise even this amount of money. In fact she begged off her first two speaking engagements, thus gaining Clay some negative publicity.

We advised Elouise to take on the attributes of a sun-sign Leo. At first she only dressed in gold colors and used Leo amulets; but soon she found this was insufficient, so she went through a private rebirth experience with us so that she could gain even more leonine characteristics.

Elouise now gathered around her a team of competent southern ladies. With her as their 'golden' leader, they gathered money the way a farmer harvests corn. When their first target was passed two weeks into the campaign, people began to take notice of what was going on. As day followed day and the flow of cash did not diminish, the newspapers started to praise Elouise statewide; Clay gained immeasurably from this reflected glory, especially when Elouise took the line that she was doing only what Clay had taught her. The contributions topped out at a little over $180,000—a figure that no one had dreamed was even remotely possible for the small community and local area. Of course Clay was re-elected; but the story does not end there.

Elouise was now so much the leader that she and Clay could no longer see eye to eye on money topics. It looked as if, in taking the leadership role, Elouise was threatening Clay's very manhood and as if their tranquil marriage might fall apart. We told Elouise in no uncertain terms that she had a choice to make: that the leonine nature which she had assumed would not last indefinitely, and that continuing with this changed nature would eventually lead to ill health. Being an intelligent woman, she consequently moderated her leadership characteristics and brought back more of her innate Libra nature. She is still a notable and quotable figure in local politics, and her marriage is serene once more. Clay now pointedly refused any requests from his aides that Elouise get out and work in support of his political career. Thus everyone is happy in his role, even if Clay may not be re-elected next time.

Astromancy Can Make You a Leader

Any leader is very little different from you or me. Just as Elouise changed herself from a shy retiring housewife into a dynamic leader, so you too can take on leadership attributes. As Ibn Saud taught, the natures that are fiery or sun-like, the Trine of Dominance from Table VII-1, are the people who will always be out leading the pack or the herd toward a goal. In Elouise' case, the goal was gold or money; so leadership toward that goal required the assumption of a Leo nature. Leadership toward other goals requires the assumption of either an Aries or a Sagittarius nature.

Table IX-1 shows which leadership characteristics you should take on for various goals. All you have to do for short-term leadership is to follow the directions in Chapter I to

Quadra of Attack	Leader in Military and Political Fields Dominance of Relationships	Red Aries ♈
Quadra of the Mirror	Leader in Patronage and Charities Acquisition of Gold	Gold Leo ♌
Quadra of Invisibility	Leader in Business and Careers Religious Leader	Blue Sagittarius ♐

Table IX-1
Trine of Domination and Leadership

acquire the nature you need. For long-term commitments you should be reborn as a natural leader, as Elouise was. Once you take on these leadership roles, you will naturally gather around you people of various other natures who will be subservient to you and will do your bidding. A natural leader will be out there leading the pack; he will need people to back him up and support him, both with good solid data and with emotional support. If you are alone, instead of support from other people you must acquire support from Astromantic energies. Once you have acquired the leadership position you need, you should learn to balance your energies as you did at the end of Chapter VIII.

Enlightened Ones Have to Lead Too

As I gaze across the vast gulf of time that doth separate me from thee, I see a great lack of spiritual leadership in all the lands. For those who are spiritually inclined do cleave to their privacy, standing not against those leaders who use leadership merely as a step toward gaining the ultimate power over lesser mortals—power which doth inevitably corrupt and destroy them. The leaders whom I see, even those in mine own land, who say they lead a new religious revival, are in no way enlightened. Their aim and lust is for power over others and they will surely be brought down by the immutable turning of the wheel of their fates. Leaders who lead only for the sake of power inevitably lead their followers and even their countries into conflict and sorrow. The time is at hand when the people will no longer allow their leaders to direct them into these negative ways; yet I do not see any enlightened ones taking up the challenge. In the marble halls of the university there are indeed great philosophers whose thoughts would change the world and make it a better place. They too must rise up and lead; for if they do not, then indeed the Armageddon that the Christians so fear will engulf us all. The enlightened ones can lead and should lead; though withal they need not give up their enlightenment.

Professor A Leads the Children to Safety

A rather interesting case of a person outside the Craft assuming a natural leadership role came to light in our recent reading about the invasion of France by the Germans in World War II. Professor A was studying Norse remnant mythology in the Normandy district of France, a part of France where Vikings held sway for many years. Those Vikings were popular among the local residents, who had previously been heavily taxed both by the church and by the state. Thus the Vikings stayed and founded dynasties; in fact it was from Normandy that the Vikings sailed when they subdued Sicily and invaded parts of Italy.

The Professor was steeped in Norse mythology, and was so intent on it that he did not pay sufficient attention to the daily news. Suddenly he found himself in a town the Germans were actually entering. He realized he must get back to England or be interned for the rest of the war—and already rumors of some of the German 'labor' camps had leaked out. He set out in his car, attempting to flee the invading forces. The Germans were still trying to prevent refugees from clogging the roads in their efforts to escape, so they were trying to bomb out various bridges along the way. In one such bombing attack a bus containing six English children and four French children had been damaged. The children had been under the supervision of a nun who was attempting to get them out of France; it was her dying wish that the Professor should take charge of the children and see them safely out of the country. Since the roads were now impassable, the Professor and the children started to walk toward the next village. In their excitement and fear, the mixed group of children was almost unmanageable, especially when they saw the death and destruction all around them. The elderly Professor had almost no inkling of how to control them; however, he remembered his Norse mythology; and when they reached the next village he obtained a long blue cloak from a bombed-out store. When he put on this blue cloak, he automatically took on the leadership role in the eyes of the children that even his adulthood had not afforded him. (It is interesting to note that as a sign of their leadership many of the ancient gods wore blue cloaks when they came to earth.)

After undergoing many adventures and gathering to himself several more children as he progressed across northern France, the Professor was able to discharge his obligations and get the children safely to England.

You Too Can Be a New Enlightened Leader

Look around you. There are hundreds and thousands of people who need leadership and guidance. Just because you are of a spiritual nature, there is no need to assume that you cannot or should not lead. As Ibn Saud has indicated, you are desperately needed in this day and age.

When you look at Table IX-1 you will see the three signs of leadership. Notice that the Sagittarius nature associated with blue is the most spiritual. This is the nature you should use to put on your blue mantle of enlightened leadership. That is not leadership which will lead you to power over others; it is leadership that will allow you to show others the path. It will not lead to gold or to power; but it will do more good in the world than any other course you could possibly pursue.

The Wind Cannot Be Shackled to the Earth

In the days of my youth, my father did make me his apprentice. As a prosperous maker of carpets, he did expect that I, his eldest son, would eventually succeed him in his business. Although I myself found great interest in the patterns as they were woven, still I found the workers had no interest in the stars that they saw each night or in the patterns that formed in the heavens above our heads. Even while their fingers created intricate designs, the workers chattered idly. My brother, my father's second son, was happy in the workshops. He could converse with the workmen and artists in a way I admired. Seeing my unhappiness, my mother did eventually persuade my father to let me journey far and study with the Sufis of Arabia. From them I gained much knowledge and a little wisdom. When my father passed on in accordance with cosmic law, I was happy to sell my share of the business to my brother in return for a small allowance which would buy my bread and sandals. Eventually I became a teacher and a leader, and found happiness therein. Under my brother's guidance the workshops did prosper; under my guidance my pupils did prosper.

Each man is fitted to a certain task, and it is thy duty to find thine allotted place, thy place of success, in this grand and mystical tapestry of life woven by the hand of the Master Allah.

Graham B Changes from Business to Church Leadership and Becomes Confidant of Presidents

Graham B lives in Minneapolis, Minnesota. Throughout his life he had been a business executive, yet he could never quite make it to the top. Although his Scorpio nature was always plotting and winning contracts and battles with his executive competitors, still enough of his very clever schemes backfired and failed to result in sales so that his record was not by any means perfect. Brilliant when the firm was in trouble, he would bring in large contracts; yet he did not bring in the routine bread-and-butter business as did his fellow sales executives. He knew he was a leader, for in his youth he won many awards for his top sales performance in such things as brushes in North Carolina. His tall stature, ash-blond hair, and piercing deep-set eyes all combined to make him a standout; yet somehow he could not succeed in business.

In a dream one night Graham realized his problem: He was a visionary leader, and the mundane business world was not for him. With this belief firmly in his head, he turned from his attempts to become a business leader and instead began preaching. Soon it was seen that he could lead throngs to enlightenment. Now as he progressed he needed Sagittarian leadership skills to keep his band together. He needed those skills as well to win the many legal conflicts that his new style of church brought on him from the government, who did not understand his ways. Today as he rides in his Cadillacs from his spacious home to his skyscraper in downtown Minneapolis, he has all a man could desire. Yet he is still driven on; for his fulfillment depends on his maintaining his leadership role.

Change Your Job to Fit Your Nature, and Win

If you are only moderately successful in your present job, it may be that you are working against your nature. There are two ways in which you can succeed.

1. You can temporarily change your nature by the Astromantic techniques we have given you; or
2. You can change your employment to fit the nature with which you were endowed at birth.

In the long run the latter choice is the better, because changing your nature can lead to internal conflict and is never satisfactory for more than a year or two. It is true that in such a time span you can achieve great things; however, a career is something which you need to be in for many years. Consequently it is best to choose carefully the best possible reconciliation between your career and your nature.

Table IX-2 shows typical leadership positions for various nativities. We recommend that you quietly examine career possibilities in your geographic area that will best fit your nature. If you are extremely water-oriented and you live in the middle of a desert, of course you should also consider moving either to a lake or to the seacoast; for you will never be truly happy until you are close to the element which is your nature.

Using the Teachings of This Chapter

The most important teaching of this chapter, a teaching which you must apply daily in your life, is that domination of other people is not necessarily an evil thing. Leaders are sadly needed in this world. To become a leader you should assume the correct leadership characteristics. When people see you put on the garb of a leader, they will automatically follow. Even people who are shy and retiring and of a spiritual nature can be, and often should be, leaders. For many leaders nowadays are in it merely for the power that it gives them—power which inevitably corrupts them. Only the spiritual leaders of this world are capable of bringing about peace and harmony.

Aquarius	Unconventional enterprises
Pisces	Police work
Aries	Military position or trial lawyer
Taurus	Farming
Gemini	Theatrical agent
Cancer	Home decorator
Leo	Fund raiser
Virgo	Retail sales
Libra	Dancer
Scorpio	Business lawyer
Sagittarius	Church leader
Capricorn	Business leader

Table IX-2
The Leadership Position for Your Nature

Sometimes it happens that people have jobs which are ill-fitted to their nature. These people have the choice of

1. changing their job; or
2. changing their nature.

The second great teaching of this chapter is that you should change your job to succeed if you are a square peg in a round career hole.

In order to win at anything, the chapter also tells you, you must choose temporarily the sign which dominates the sign of the person or the object that you wish to govern. The Wheel of Mastery in the first section of this chapter is a most powerful tool; it will insure your success over others in all matters when domination is your way to success.

Chapter Ten

REAPING A HARVEST OF RICHES WITH ASTROMANCY

What This Chapter Will Do for You

There are more than 525,000 millionaires in the United States. That is, one in every 400 people is a millionaire. This chapter is designed to help you achieve that status. First, however, it will help you to:

- Remove Your Debts
- Win at Games of Chance
- Gain an Inheritance
- Earn More
- Find Buried Treasure

The Immutable Law of Attraction

Thou must understand that things of like nature attract one another. When thou hast a pile of shekels, more will automatically be attracted unto it. If thou hast a large rug-making business, if it is in thy nature, that business will expand for thee. In my land when a father did start such a business from his own natural desires, it expanded so rapidly that all were amazed by it. His son, who perhaps had not the nature for such a business enterprise, added his nature unto it and brought it to ruin. From this we learn that all is ordained as it should be. The nature of some is to gain shekels, of others to expand businesses, and of yet others to spend. The nature of some is to become money lenders, of some to labor in the fields; and of others to fish in the wide oceans of the world. If Allah had not ordained the world this way in His wisdom, then naught could be accomplished, for all would wish to do the least work for the most shekels. It is the nature of some to gain wealth by working in the counting house, and it is the nature of others to gain wealth by gathering camel dung for fertilizer and fuel. It is natural for the father to wish his son to follow him in his business, and for his son to follow him until the end of time. Yet unless the nature of these sons be such that they would bring prosperity to the business, it would be better for the father to employ a stranger to run it rather than one of his own kin who hath a nature unsuited to the work. Times without number I have seen in my long life the futile attempts of those who should be gathering dung as they persist in trying to gain wealth through employment in the counting houses.

Certain natures attract wealth; and thou canst put on the visage of such a nature. The gathering of wealth is an effort which requireth many revolutions of the Wheel of the Heavens; thou shouldst thus consider a long span of time for the effort. Also thou must look into thine own nature and decide whether thou mayest gain greater wealth by using thine own nature to best advantage.

Bankrupt Cynthia Finds Wealth

Student File 2G-6DR

For as long as she could remember, our student Cynthia O who lived in Columbia, South Carolina, had been told that when she got to her 25th birthday she would get a large inheritance from her grandmother. From knowing that she had this inheritance coming, she planned her life around having her own dress shop. As much as her Gemini nature would allow, she fitted herself for this future dream by taking all sorts of college courses in such light fields as silk screening, fine arts, and window dressing. . . . Yet even in the courses she took she really just skimmed the surface. She did not get involved in depth in anything; and as to getting into dull things like accounting and management, these she felt she could well do without. In order to round out her education she borrowed money on the strength of her inheritance-to-be and flitted around Europe for a year, seeing what was selling and what the 'latest' ideas were in Paris and Rome. She came back to Columbia with the fixed intent of showing the women of the city what they should wear.

As soon as she got her hands on her inheritance, Cynthia leased a store and stocked it with the very latest in fashionable wear. But her nature was such that she could never rest content that her stock was 'right.' Even the few good customers she had became confused with her sudden switches in recommendations as to what was being worn this season around the world. Of course she was too utterly bored, my dear, with the day-to-day management of the business; and she left this to a rather incompetent young woman whom she had met at a party.

Trouble was not long in coming. It took three years for Cynthia to spend her grandmother's inheritance and also bankrupt herself. She was nearly destitute, and yet too proud to go back and live with her parents. At this point, as many do in their desperation, she wrote to us and asked for a money spell. After we talked with her via letters for several weeks, we told her that what she needed was not a money spell but a different type of occupation; for her Gemini nature meant she could gain great wealth by being a go-between or a matchmaker and she should never have gotten herself tied down into a business as she had done.

During her time in the store she had observed that most sales representatives from the fashion houses gave the impression of being ill-informed and rather boring. The one rep who stood out in her memory had gained rapid promotion in his firm. Following our advice, Cynthia called him and asked for a job. He immediately agreed to this request because he had both a soft spot for Cynthia and a sales territory available.

Cynthia immediately prospered. She outsold all the other sales people in the firm. She was doing the thing her nature required of her; that was, bringing together the company's products and its customers. Nowadays she is not only considered by the firm one of its most able sales people, but also is trusted by them to travel to Europe and advise on their whole fashionable dress line.

Your Way to Natural Riches

As Cynthia's example shows, it may not be your fault that you are not gaining the wealth and riches you expect from the world. Your natural energies will allow you to gain wealth in one particular natural way. In Chapter IX, Table IX-2 shows the careers best suited to each nature. Look at your nature and see whether the work you are presently doing will lead you to the best careers, or whether you can slightly modify the work you are doing to get it more in line with your nature. If you find that you have a mismatch in your life, yet you like your present work and can see some prospect of success in it, you should follow the long-term technique given in Chapter III to take on the attributes of the nature which will allow you to succeed in your present job.

This will make you tremendously more successful in your immediate endeavors.

If you are not content with this, you should also start looking for a career that will be natural to you. In this way you will not only gain much wealth, but you will also be far happier in your work; for you will not be forcing yourself out of your natural inborn pattern of talents. We do not recommend that you immediately give up your present employment and launch out into a new career without adequate preparation. We do recommend that you start looking and preparing for a new career, and at the same time you put on the guise that will best reconcile your nature with your present career. For this purpose you may use a rebirth procedure as recommended in Chapter V, or you may wear properly colored clothes in colors which are suited to the task.

Lastly, of course, we strongly recommend that you always bring a little Sagittarius luck and nature into your work. Write all your notes, if you like, with a dark blue pen; and every time you see the blue color flowing from its point remember that the blue is bringing you luck and success.

Do Not Scatter Thy Forces

The competent farmer as he tills his fields plants large areas of single crops. Assuredly, near his home he plants a varied garden so that he can provide his family with many various fruits and vegetables; but his main purpose is the raising of a single crop. When this crop hath need of work, he doth not spend time in his family garden. His main crop receiveth all his attention. He doth not scatter his energies and dissipate his forces in raising many different crops each of which would require specialized knowledge, attention, and equipment. When he worketh he doth one task alone and doth it correctly.

If thou art to succeed in any task in thy life, thou must emulate the farmer. Set thy mind and all thine efforts unto a single task which is part of the grand scheme that thou hast plotted for thy life; then thou wilt assuredly succeed. ***I*** *have seen with mine own eyes how some farmers of the village having but one pair of camels, a handful of chickens, and some wheat do fail because, unlike their more astute brethren, they labor from morning till night first feeding one animal, then tending another, then gathering their small crop—and yet withal they make no profit. Other farmers may get up as the sun breaketh over the land to tend their flocks, but then they are to be found smoking around the well for the rest of the day. Their single task is soon completed; and when they count their shekels, these men have many to bury under their poor-looking huts.*

Walter Works Less for More

Student File 2Y-6WA

Walter H lives in a small town north of Los Angeles. Of all the people who ever wrote to us to join our School, Walter's life was financially the most chaotic we have ever come across. Yet he came from a relatively wealthy family. His grandfather was a multi-millionaire, but his father was what used to be called a 'wastrel.' He had died at an early age in a plane crash when he had attempted to fly through a Sierra mountain pass for a small wager. Grandpa H doted on his grandson; and after the problems he had had with his own son, he was extremely careful not to spoil the boy. However, it was through his attitude that Walter had gotten himself into the financial jam that caused him to write to us for help.

For many years Walter had been a biker and had enjoyed the life around the tracks. He had joined many of his friends in the very positive group actions that various bike clubs undertake. His grandfather did not like him to ride on the street on a bike, so he made a down payment on an Aston Martin sports car for him. Since Grandpa was 'not going to spoil the boy', he insisted that Walter keep up the payments on the car. Since the car cost close to $20,000 even after Grandfather's one-third down, still the payments were astronomical: so much so in fact that when it came time to renew the insurance on the car after the first year, Walter just didn't have the money; and even when the finance company wrote to say they would withdraw the loan, still he made excuses as to why he could not pay the insurance. The disaster which really started Walter's financial ruin then happened. He wrecked his car. Now the finance company came after him in earnest, but agreed not to sue provided he would quickly pay off the loan. Walter's grandfather at this time was getting to be a very old man, not expected to live very long; and Walter was scared of taking his troubles to him for fear the old man would cut him out of his will because he felt Walter was following the same path his father had gone down.

In order to pay the finance company and to have enough money over to live, Walter ended up taking three jobs. He sold appliances at Zody's; he moonlighted as a bartender; and he was also active as a door-to-door representative for a portrait photographer. He slept very little; he ate very little; he had no spare time—yet he had no success. For he did not achieve any great sales record either with the photography or with Zody's, and he made a very dull bartender. He lived in constant fear of losing one of his jobs, and this attitude too caused him to perform poorly. Again, when Walter asked us for a money spell, we did not do one. Instead, we instructed him in doing a spell that would get him a job more suited to his nature: a job that would help him eliminate his debts. These both came under the sign of Aquarius.

We were not surprised when Walter wrote to tell us that an old friend from his biker days had offered him a sales job in his new store provided that Walter would ride on the local track circuit for him. Not only did he ride well, he also won! With these winnings he was able to pay off the car finance company.

Currently Walter is a happy partner in the store, a position that he gained through his own nature. His grandfather did indeed leave Walter a considerable fortune; however, he has not had to touch a penny of it. He is both out of debt and content in the sales job that brings him more than enough money for his needs.

Whirling Your Scattered Forces into a Whole

Many people grow up with a preconceived notion of what job would suit them best. They try one job and find it does not suit them, then another; and so they go from one job to another and by a wasteful, time-consuming process of elimination eventually find something they like fairly well to do. Using your Career Table, Table IX-2, you can start with a significant advantage over these people. You instantly know the type of career which will bring you the most success. Now all you have to do is focus and concentrate your attention on that particular career. If you do this properly, the career opportunities you want will come to you. Yes, of course you may have to answer a few ads and prepare yourself for your future position as a leader and for the wealth it will bring you. Any device which concentrates your attention will help. Focusing on a colored candle is one that is often recommended. We, however, like to be more active than that; and a device which we have found most effective is a simple button on a string.

Figure X-1 shows such a device. All you have to do is take a button, run a loop of string through the holes, and hold the ends of the loop between them and the fingers of the right and left hands. With slack in the loop, swing the button around so that the string becomes twisted. Now pull the hands apart so that the twist in the string makes the button spin. With an easy rhythmic motion of the hands in and out, you can make the button spin in both directions and keep it spinning at any speed you like. Table X-1 shows you the color of button you should use for each career opportunity, whether you should spin it quickly or slowly, and for how long at a stretch you should concentrate on it. You should do this simple exercise when you get up in the morning and just before you finally go to sleep at night. Concentrate with all your intensity on the career you wish and on the whirling button. If you get career ideas while you are watching the button whirl

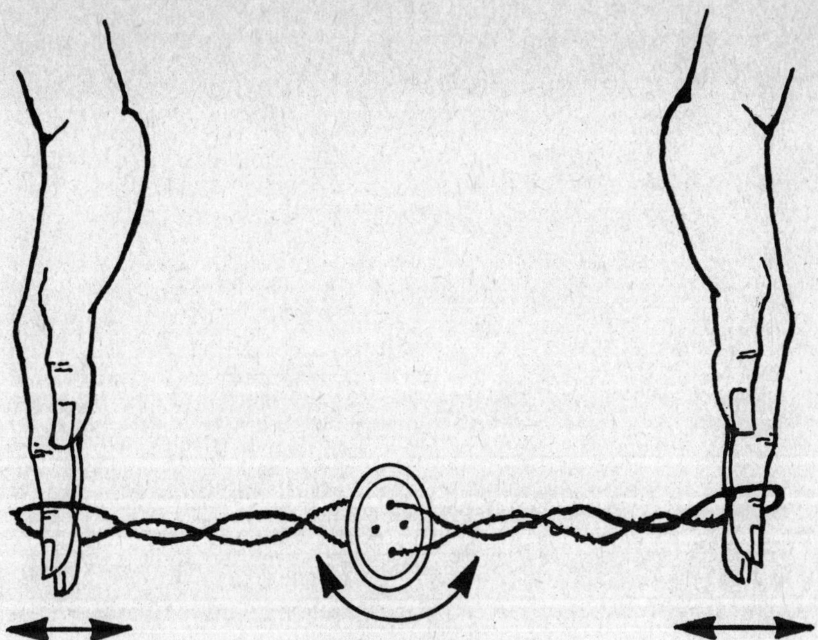

Figure X-1
Your Whirling Disk of Success

or during the night, do not hesitate to follow up on them; for these are the ideas that will eventually lead to your new successful leadership career.

Look to the Wheel of the Heavens for Aid

Whatever thou desirest, thou canst find it if thou but lookest unto the Heavenly Wheel above thy head. If thou holdest in thy hand a treasure map, assuredly there are energies like unto the Ram that will help thee find thy treasure. If thou art in debt to the moneylender, thou canst achieve freedom from thy indebtedness by using other energies. All is in its appointed place as Allah did will it. Do not rail against misfortune if in thine ignorance thou hast failed to use that which Allah did lay to hand for all to benefit from. But if thou sittest in thy hut and workest not, even though kindly villagers may feed thee from charity, still thou wilt never achieve greatness. Thou must take steps to achieve thy desires. Thou canst take these steps in a proper direction, always proceeding toward thy dreamed-of oasis; and this will save thee much labor. But if thou dost not take the first step, thou wilt never succeed.

Career Wanted	Color of Button	Spin Speed	Length of Time In Minutes
Unconventional	Violet	Very Fast	5
Police Work	Lavender	Fast	7
Military Leader, Trial Lawyer	Scarlet	Medium	9
Farmer	Brown/Red	Slow	13
Theatrical Agent	Yellow	Very Fast	5
Home Decorator	Amber	Fast	7
Fund Raiser	Gold	Medium	9
Retail Sales	Chartreuse	Slow	13
Dancer	Green	Very Fast	5
Business Lawyer	Turquoise	Fast	7
Church Leader	Blue	Medium	9
Business Leader	Indigo	Slow	13

Table X-1
Parameters for Making and Using Your Whirling Disk

Marvin's Trip to a Quarter-Million Dollars

Student File 2Y-2TN

Marvin G used to live in a furnished apartment in Compton, California. He was a typical aircraft mechanic, a skilled riveter, earning enough to get by, drifting along with the crowd. His Pisces nature accepted this state of affairs which he thought was right for one of his mixed German-Spanish heritage. The German part of him told him that you got ahead by good work; and the Spanish Pisces nature encouraged him to live one day at a time, for mañana things would be better. He was taking our course; but even in this he drifted along.

One day he did an inheritance money procedure for himself, even though, as far as any of us knew, no inheritance was even dreamed of for him. Still, as he said, "I just felt like doing it, so I did it." Soon after that he wrote us a very complaining letter saying it hadn't worked. The only thing he had gotten as a result of it was a letter from a lawyer in Germany saying that he had been left two small lots in a Bavarian city. Having spent time in Germany, Yvonne and I both knew that a German lawyer's 'two small lots' might represent a fortune by American standards. It took a great deal of persuasion, but finally we got Marvin to write to the lawyer for a specific description of the land and for a description of the steps he would have to take to convert these lots into cash. It turned out that the two small lots were in fact a full hectare (just under 2½ acres) in downtown Ulm! Marvin was still not very excited about this, especially because the lawyers told him the best way to convert the land to cash was to come and spend a month or so in Ulm. Of course his view of land prices was colored by the (at that time) low prices that one could expect for property in and around Compton. Nothing we could do by letter would persuade Marvin to change his mind. We even told him that as a Pisces he should expect that any fortune he was to gain would come by crossing water.

As part of our course we encourage students to investigate other religions and check out the available fringe churches around them, for we do not wish people to espouse Witchcraft merely as a rebound religion when they get upset with Christianity. Marvin went to a local spiritualist church to fulfill this assignment. He was totally freaked out when the minister told him that she saw the spirit of a serious German gentleman who was a relative and who was extremely upset with Marvin for not taking his inheritance seriously. Between this experience and our letters, Marvin finally convinced himself that he should take the steps to go to Germany. He managed with our our prompting to get himself a passport and tickets, and much to our surprise he even took a German language course. When he got to Germany the lawyer made no bones with him about what the lots would fetch on the market. Ulm had become an extremely prosperous city, especially since the Telefunken company had made it their new headquarters. Finally the lawyer himself bought one of the lots and the other was quickly sold to a new supermarket chain. Marvin brought back over a million Deutschmarks which at that time were worth over a quarter-million dollars.

Marvin was so pleased with the results of his first spell that he did another. This had the seemingly peculiar result of delaying payment of some 600,000 DM. He wrote to us in a great huff, forgetting all the previous gain he had made, saying that he was now sure that Astromancy did not work. Not two months later the German government revalued the DM, from 4 to the dollar to 2 to the dollar; thus Marvin's 600,000 DM ($150,000) overnight became $300,000. Needless to say, his faith in Astromancy was restored.

Your Astromantic Wheel of Wealth

Whatever avenue you wish to follow to gain wealth, there is a nature and a sign appropriate to it. These are identified in Figure X-2. Marvin used the gain-by-inheritance nature to bring to himself many hundreds of thousands of dollars. You can use various natures to aid you in your daily life.

The trine of natures that most quickly bring in money are shown in Table X-2. These are the ones you should first use in working toward great wealth. Table X-2 also shows the quadra to which each of the trine natures belongs, so that you may work in ways harmonious with each respective quadra.

	Aries	Leo	Sagittarius
	Find Treasure (Salvage)	Leadership	Winning
Quadra	Attack	Mirror	Invisibility

Table X-2
Your Trine of Wealth Natures

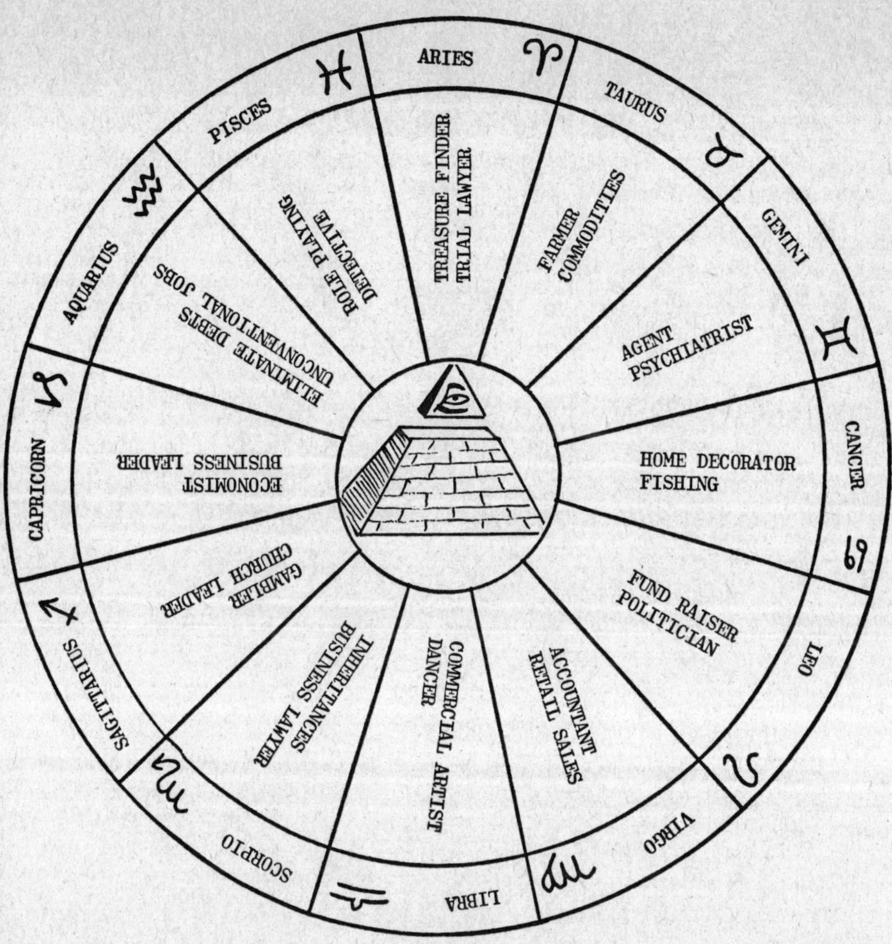

Figure X-2
Your Astromantic Wheel of Wealth

- **Aries—Wealth by finding treasure**

This may be the historic-type buried treasure; it might also be the overlooked opportunity for gain that is hidden in such tasks as salvaging and renovating old cars or buildings. The attack quadra is fulfilled when you go out and aggressively purchase these salvable items.

• **Leo—Wealth from leadership**

The good leader reflects the wishes of the group. After assuming the Leo nature, you must form the group to be led. Easiest is a charitable organization: an appeal for funds for the last, most worthy cause. Whether it be an earthquake in Greece or children in Nicaragua, still funds will pour in. The Leo nature is honest and upright, and will assure everyone that more of the funds will do good than in most charities.

• **Sagittarius—Wealth by winning**

No matter what you wish to win at, this nature brings you the energy that will assure your success. Be invisible while you win, and you will not lose your funds to a hungry government or to friends and acquaintances.

Gaining wealth by these means is not a short-term undertaking, so you should use the procedure in Chapter III.

There is one last nature that may be most useful to you at this time. That is Aquarius of the mirror quadra. The Aquarian nature is the one best suited to getting out of debt. Assume this nature, and by doing all the unconventional things you can think of you will automatically erase your debts.

Evil Is Not in Riches

It is assuredly true that on occasion lowly people have done great good. However, it is far easier for a man of wealth to pursue spiritual truth than it is for the son of a lowly carpenter. The Prophet Himself was not successful until he attained sufficient wealth through his marriage to lay aside the everyday cares of acquiring food and shelter. The Buddha, probably the greatest spiritual leader apart from Allah's Prophet Mohammed, was himself a prince before he laid aside the pleasures of that life to bring happiness and spiritual awareness to countless millions of the unenlightened. How can a dung-collector become known and how indeed can he be accepted in the halls of princes? His words must indeed be more than inspired, and he must perform countless magics before he gathereth to himself followers. How too can he understand the spirituality that the rich man doth need in as great a measure as his less fortunate brother mortal? Surely it is easier for the rich man to learn of the poor than it is for the poor to learn of the rich.

Allah in His wisdom gave us poor humans certain basic drives. The most basic is to survive. The man without water lost in the desert still strives onward. The man without food lost in the city steals to eat. Thus doth poverty engender evil (if stealing for food can be called by that name). For as thou wilt find on thy travel through the world, evil lieth not in mere thievery but in ignorance of the great Wheel of the Heavens and of the purpose of Life itself.

Heiress Myrna Finds Happiness

Student File 6G-4EJ

Myrna E is still a very wealthy woman. Nowadays she is serene in her wealth though that was not always the case. When we met her she was dour, distrustful, and crippled up with arthritis. Myrna was born with the proverbial silver spoon in her mouth. Her father had made millions in Colorado silver mining, and when he died she was his only heir. Her first marriage in college she thought was for love; but it turned out that the boy she married was interested only in her money. Almost as soon as they were married he began playing around and had little time for her. Finally in a bitter quarrel one night he told her outright that he had married her for her money. In those days before the first World War, being a girl in college was somewhat unusual; and getting a divorce was a long and difficult procedure which resulted in lasting social disgrace, especially since Myrna was left with twin daughters as a result of the encounter. Yes, she learned from her first love affair, but she was lonely; and when another likable young man wooed her, she fell again for his line. This marriage, it is true, lasted almost ten years; but again at the end the truth came out and money was the problem. This last emotional breakup finally convinced Myrna that all men were only after her money. Even Myrna's Aquarian nature could not save her from deep despondency, as her two divorces had made her a total outcast from her social set. Her relatives even got to her children and gradually the children became little monsters, not responding to their mother's attempts at discipline; after all, who was she to discipline them?

The older she grew, the more embittered she became. She became the archetypal crochety, miserly, older woman, living only for herself and clutching everything to herself. She went out less and less; and, perhaps as an excuse for this, she became a victim of crippling arthritis. People began to call her the "witch on the hill." Probably motivated mainly by hate and by her nickname, Myrna wrote to us and asked to take our course. (In those days we were occasionally able to give courses to deserving people without charge. Nowadays, when we do not charge, we usually insist on some goods or services in exchange for the course.)

Myrna told us that she had no money and we believed her. She was utterly amazed that anyone would give anything away free, especially religious teachings; because in the past in her troubles she had tried various churches. It had seemed to her that all without exception were more interested in her wealth than in her spiritual serenity. Anyway after the first couple of lectures Myrna paid us in full for the course. She attended several of our semiannual seminars and found, much to her surprise, that most of the people at the seminars were altogether uninterested in money and in fact would share what little they had with her, often in preference to going with her to a restaurant. This view of the world, which was totally different than anything she had previously experienced and yet still appealed strongly to her Aquarian nature, brought her back into the mainstream of life with a rush. She met, and from time to time lived with, two or three older gentlemen who lived the Craft. Finally after much experimentation she married one of them; and though they are not now of the Craft but have opened their own spiritual retreat in California, still Myrna is content using her money to raise the awareness of others; and by teaching this raised awareness she is gaining much spiritual wealth. The need for her arthritis long ago disappeared, and her arthritis itself went away with the need. She is quite contented now, a lovely person whom her children finally understand and respect.

Riches of the Spirit World

Gaining wealth often brings problems with it. The popular stereotype of the lonely death of the eccentric millionaire or the executive's dramatic suicide is based in fact. When you gain great riches, as you most easily can, you often give up spiritual wealth. Many so-called spiritual teachers are poor people who make their living trying to raise the awareness of others; however, their path has in it strong elements of materialism and you should be careful when you take them for a teacher. For how can a person whose whole object in life is the gaining of wealth teach the higher spiritual truths? Even the hermit who lives in his cell does not make a good spiritual teacher; for knowing little of the world, he does not understand your mundane problems. By isolating himself from these problems, his spirit atrophies and his teachings get set into those which are applicable to the time when he left the world. You yourself must achieve the balance of the Wheel of the Heavens. There is a time when you must place emphasis on gaining wealth; there is a time when you should use that wealth to balance your life through the gaining of spiritual riches.

When you gain great wealth, you should balance that by great spiritual awareness. For a complete person, the two go hand in hand. There is no evil in gaining great wealth unless you accompany that with a total rejection of all spiritual knowledge and of humanity, compassion, and understanding. Yes, you can try the 'hard' path. Yes, you can live on less. But the people we have spoken to who have tried this path seem to us to have a hardness in their spiritual awareness which allows them to accept none but their own rather narrow truths.

Hunger encourages crime just as drug addiction does.

The addict will do anything to get the money to support his habit. In the final instance, you will do anything to feed yourself or your children. This is not the way to spiritual development. This is not the way to greatness. We urge you to establish yourself comfortably before you attempt to gain sainthood.

Putting the Knowledge of This Chapter to Use in Your Life

Yes indeed, you must plan and work a little if you wish to become as rich as the legendary king Croesus. The following steps should help you on your way.

1. Select a career that is in tune with your nature. Look at the table and disk that we provide for you in Figure X-1 and Table X-1. Select from them the path that will lead to success and wealth.

2. Prepare yourself both for the new career and for the riches it will bring while you use your whirling disk to bring everything together and make that career come true for you.

3. Do not overlook the possibility that your mate or lover has a career potential greater than your own. So complete these same steps for your partner. If it turns out that your partner has a higher potential, then support that partner in efforts toward the chosen career.

4. Many careers require initial investments. You can use your Wheel of Wealth to aid you in winning short-term gains so that you can be ready when opportunity knocks. Similarly, you can improve your present job income and position by using techniques which will make you naturally more suited to that job.

Whatever you do, do not sit idly by and let drift away the golden opportunities to become another millionaire which we have presented to you.

Chapter Eleven

CHANGING YOUR LUCK WITH ASTROMANCY

What This Chapter Can Do for You

The techniques previously described in this book will reshape your life. Some people, however, just are certain that whatever they do, bad luck will dog their heels and nothing will improve their life. This chapter will change all that for you. It will change bad luck to good, and additionally show you how to

- Overcome Hexes and Negative Predictions
- Gain Your Own Lucky Charm or Mojo
- Find Your Own Lucky Number
- Win:

- The girl of your dreams
- The game of chance
- Wealth

Hiding Thy Light under a Bushel

If thou livest always in thy same accustomed round, never venturing aught, thou needest not any better luck than thou now hast; however, when thou becomest dissatisfied with thy mundane existence and venturest out into the world, thou must assuredly take with thee a little more than thine own natural skills and the skills for changing thy nature which I have taught thee. If thou hast not a modicum of that indefinable thing the sages call "Luck" with thee, all thy good works and great qualities may not gain thee the oasis of thy dreams. Fortunately in ancient times the Watchers noted that one nature was blessed beyond others and seemingly was touched by the finger of the Goddess of Good Fortune. Thus it is that nowadays we can show thee how thou canst avail thyself of a portion of these blessings. But withal, if thou dost never leave thy humble shack thou canst not expect that these blessings will abide with thee. They are given only to those who do venture into the world and like a shining beacon lead others onward to bright and beautiful destinies.

Karl Turns His Luck Around and Becomes a Millionaire

Student File 2Y-8DL

Karl P lives as he always has in New York City. His grandfather made a fortune in cooperage; that is, the making of barrels. His father continued and expanded the profitable business, but it was not in Karl's nature to be a dynamic businessman. He was a Pisces. His nature was like that of a Fish and his Quadra was that of Invisibility.

There is an old saying in Europe: "Clogs to clogs in three

generations." That is, a dynamic man from a family too poor to wear proper shoes will found a business; the son will continue it—and the grandson will squander the earned wealth, rendering the family once more unable to afford any shoes better than clogs. It seemed as if Karl was a perfect illustration of this saying. In fact his father was fond of quoting it to him. Of course the more his father expected him to fail and to squander the money, the more Karl did in fact fail and squander. Karl's whole life seemed fraught with failure. He married young, mostly to get away from his domineering father; and his marriage rapidly deteriorated and fell apart. With his fish-like nature, Karl was not overly concerned by the continuous disasters in his life. He just drifted along, not worrying about them. Perhaps he thoroughly believed that, as his father had so often told him, he was foredoomed to be a wastrel and a failure.

In a moment of idleness, Karl wrote to us to take our course. In it he learned of the differing natures of people, and learned that Luck was something one could gain just as one gained money. At one of our seminars, Karl met a dynamic young Arian lady and determined he would win her. Even though we warned him that his nature was incompatible with hers, he determined to change himself to a compatible Sagittarian nature, changing to her trine but remaining in his own Quadra. Karl's whole life changed. The day after he had his rebirth experience, he won a grand prize in the Irish Sweepstakes. Suddenly Karl was a winner, not a loser. Everything he touched was good for him. It didn't seem to matter whether he went to the racetrack, bet on a lottery, or invested in property; whatever he did made a profit. Not only that, but with his new luck and prosperity Karl found many new companions, and very soon he was the young playboy about town.

Gradually, of course, he reverted to his old nature; and as he reverted, so his luck flowed away from him again. In his period of good luck, he had totally forgotten about the course he was taking from us; for he had been far too busy to work on it. Karl is a very intelligent man, however; and when he saw his luck changing again he wrote to us to ask us why this was. We pointed out that in his quest for the Arian lady he had changed his nature to that of the most luck and that now his nature was reverting and his luck was ebbing with it. We were able to show him how he could be himself and yet retain most of the luck that he enjoyed when he was reborn as a Sagittarius.

Karl has not yet remarried. But he is a multi-millionaire and has many companions, all because he changed his luck and took advantage of that change.

Gain Luck and Laugh at Negative Predictions

Ibn Saud clearly stated that one particular nature had more luck than any other. That nature is Sagittarius. It is the nature which sees out the old harvest year, for it is the nature which occurs just before winter solstice. The closer we get to winter solstice, December 21 or 22, the more luck the Sagittarian nature brings to itself; and in the last decan (ten-day period) before winter solstice, all the luck of the world seems to flow to it. When you are in need of luck, you must call on this specific decan of the Sagittarian nature. When Karl went through his rebirth cycle, he came out as a *late* Sagittarius.

If you are by birth of this decan, that is, your birthdate is between December 12 and 21, and still you do not have good luck, it is because in your younger days you ignored the luck that came to you. In order to regain the luck you lost, you should go through a 24-hour rebirth cycle, bringing yourself back and being reborn exactly on your own birthdate.

In order to bring to yourself just a small portion of this Sagittarian nature, you can do such things as wear dark blue clothing, wear sapphires of the darkest blue you can obtain, eat asparagus, and drink warmed drinks to which a little nutmeg has been added. All these things will bring luck to you. Again, we would like to repeat Ibn Saud's warnings: If you stay home and do nothing, then no amount of luck will help you. You must get out into the world and use your natural ability together with the luck which being reborn in the last decan of Sagittarius will bring you.

As Day Followeth Night, So Doth Good Luck Follow Bad

Allah in His wisdom keepeth all things in balance. Look unto the heavens and see how in every direction thou lookest there are stars and planets in abundance. Thus it is in life. Assuredly there are dark times, but always beyond the darkness there are many beckoning welcoming lights. If thou but usest a little energy and intelligence thou canst reach those lights. All is in balance. If today thou hast bad luck in the marketplace, assuredly tomorrow thou wilt find thy luck taking a change for the better. If thou proceedest down a dark tunnel, luck may run against thee for several months. This is where thou must change thy nature, for by changing thy nature thou wilt direct thy footsteps back into the light, breaking out of thy tunnel of despair and ill fortune.

Mayhap thou hast noted that in the hour before dawn thou art attacked by pangs of despair but after the dawn happiness and good cheer come to thee. This change of thy nature occurreth every morning of thy life. If thou wishest to change thy life, thou must of course change thy nature. The energies from beyond the stars are there for thy use and benefit. These energies are absorbed and retained by the things that are around thee in thy dwelling. They are even absorbed by thy trappings and by the baubles that thou wearest. Thus it is assuredly true that when the Goddess of Good Fortune doth smile upon thee with special favor, thou shouldst keep the trappings and the baubles thou didst wear on that occasion. When thou wearest them again, they will ever more remind thee of and give the energy of the great good fortune which thou didst enjoy in that happy moment. It will ever more be thine while thou dost keep about thee those trappings and baubles.

Beware, though, lest thou destroyest the good fortune of these accoutrements by overly using the energies which they contain; for even these energies can be exhausted by overuse. In order to recharge and revitalize these accoutrements, thou must be reborn with them into thy special time of thy blessing.

Grandma's Bequest Brings Yetta Diamonds and Contentment

A reporter from a New York City newspaper was interviewing us, and one of the stories we told about luck reminded him of the following incident.

Yetta H is the youngest daughter of a New York diamond merchant. In the family tradition, a daughter is supposed to stay at home and become a good housekeeper. Yetta had an Arian nature, however, and she wanted to be just as successful in the business world as the male members of her family had been before her. She started a secretarial service, catering especially to the diamond merchants and to other members of the Jewish community. As the daughter of a well-known family, she felt that the diamond merchants would trust her with their custom. But tradition dies hard, and she found that her path was not an easy one. Yetta did not worry when her business got into difficulties, mainly because her aged grandmother had always told her that when she died she was going to leave her most valuable possession to Yetta. Somehow in Yetta's mind this unspecified bequest had become several sacks of diamonds worth many hundreds of thousands, even millions, of dollars.

Yetta 'knew' that no matter what happened, even if she lost everything in her foundering business, still she would be all right; so she borrowed money on her expectations and really got herself into a non-win situation. When Grandmother died Yetta was really in desperate straits and her heart was beating fast as she opened the leather package that was her bequest. She was horrified to find within it only a very old necklace set with what she recognized as sapphire chips. The whole value of the bequest was probably less than $100. Yetta was extremely disappointed, of course, for her grandmother had made a generous bequest of valuable diamonds to Yetta's brother. Nevertheless, out of love and respect for her grandmother, Yetta wore her bequest to the funeral.

From that hour Yetta's life changed. At the funeral she met another young adult who was also trying to break out of his family's diamond-merchant tradition. It was a love affair at first sight. When Yetta and Herschel combined their strengths, her business and his book-publishing concern both prospered. Today Yetta still wears her grandmother's necklace when she feels things are going against her; and she has both diamonds in her jewel box and contentment in a secure home and business.

Finding Your Own Lucky Piece or 'Mojo'

There are two basic ways that you can get your own equivalent of Yetta's good-luck necklace.

1. You can remember the last time you had good fortune, and when you next need good luck wear the clothes and jewelry that you had on at that time.

2. You can make your own good-luck talisman.[1] Start with the design of the Sagittarian disk in Chapter I; this should be engraved either on a piece of pure tin or on a piece of wood cut from a thorny locust tree. On the back you should have engraved the letters I*O*M, which mean "Jupiter Omnis Magnus"; for Jupiter is the god and Jupiter is the planet which bring luck.

---

[1]For complete details of making and fine-tuning amulets and talismans, read Gavin and Yvonne's "Witch's Grimoire of Ancient Omens, Portents, Talismans, Amulets, and Charms" available from Parker Publishing.

In most cases a lucky talisman such as the left hind foot of a white rabbit has power of and by itself, so it does not need charming; but because charming does no harm, any time you feel doubt that the talisman is truly connected to the lucky energy pool, it should be charmed. In general there are three steps required for the proper charming of any object.

Step 1—Psychically cleansing the object. This is accomplished in one of two ways.

A. Boil the object in salted water while you recite aloud the Abracadabra diminishing ritual shown in Figure XI-1; then plunge the object into cold water.

B. Heat the object in an oven to 250°F; then take it out and place it on a block of ice while you recite the diminishing ritual.

A B R A C A D A B R A

A B R A C A D A B R

A B R A C A D A B

A B R A C A D A

A B R A C A D

A B R A C A

A B R A C

A B R A

A B R

A B

A

Figure XI-1
Diminishing Ritual

It is the thermal shock that releases any psychic power latent in the object. Going into the water or the melted ice, the power can safely be washed away.

Step 2—Selecting the place and time for your charming. Sorcerers and Witches go to great lengths to be sure they do their work at the correct time and place. At your present level of development, adequate charming can be obtained by remembering a couple of simple rules.

A. Time: New moon overhead.

B. Place: A high place like a mountain or a hilltop or the top of a building.

Step 3—The actual charming. The object has been made. You have cleansed it. You should buy a dark blue candle and a piece of dark blue cotton fabric. When you have these things, at high noon on the day of the new moon, place the amulet on the cloth and light the candle by the side of it. Remove all your clothing, all rings, jewelry, hairpins, and body bindings, so that you are totally unbound. Concentrate on the lighted candle, thinking thoughts of what you desire as intently as you can. Hold this position until the candle begins to flicker in your mind; this should take perhaps five minutes. Now begin to chant repetitively, "Aye-Oh-Em." Your chant should start softly and gradually rise in volume until it is a shout. You will probably repeat the syllables about fifty times before screaming at the climax, "Luck to me!" and with the scream clapping your hands violently in the candle flame so as to extinguish it.

Your talisman is now charged; when you are not wearing it, you should keep it wrapped with the candle in the cloth you used in the charging ritual. These energies are not inexhaustible, however; and you will want to recharge your talisman any time your luck seems to be running out.

In order to help you get a feeling for the way the chant should sound, we would encourage you to listen to a recording of "Old McDonald's Farm," especially the repetition of the phrase "ee-aye, ee-aye, oh." The repetition and the building of volume, speed, and intensity are all vital to the building of an effective charm. We suspect that "Old McDonald's Farm" is in fact an ancient pagan chant that was once used to bless and charm all the living creatures on the farm, now translated into modern form. You should practice this method of building volume, power, and intensity before you charm your first talisman. Once you have the knack, however, it is simplicity itself.

The Future Buildeth on the Past

If thou hadst not been born, thou wouldst have no life and no problems. Hadst thou been born unto a great sheik, it is likely thou wouldst have all thy heart could desire. As thou progressest through thy life, thou must constantly look over thy shoulder to see that thou dost progress on an ascending spiral of wealth. Here I must say that wealth is not measured only in the number of shekels thou hast hidden away, but is measured also in the quality of thy companions and in thy spiritual growth. Wealth must withal be understood to be a combination of all *the wealth in thy life, not merely the gold. The seeds of tomorrow are assuredly cast into the ground today. Thine actions today will bear fruit tomorrow. If thou castest no seed into the soil, thou canst reap no reward. What is true in thy life and in the world is true in the heavens; for doth not the sun rise only after it hath set? Luck too doth build as doth thy life, and if it is to flourish it must be nurtured as is the seedling. When thou hast luck, remember it so that thou mayest build on that luck and gain yet more good fortune.*

Loser Orval Becomes Lucky Harry

Orval M is a racehorse handicapper: what we used to call a tipster. In choosing this profession he was not only following in his father's footsteps; he also really loved racehorses and the whole racing milieu. Now a good handicapper first analyzes the horses in the race to see which is likely to win; then he uses his psychic ability to choose between the most likely candidates to pick the ultimate winner. It is this final step that defies formal mathematical analysis—and it is this step that Orval was wholly unable to master. He knew his horseflesh; he knew his jockeys; and he knew his tracks. He could always get within one or two horses of the winner. But that final touch of genius, that psychic ability which enables the good handicapper regularly to select winners, just was not in Orval. Time and again his father would let him back his judgment; and time and again Orval lost. Though his father had the gift, he just couldn't explain to Orval how to 'get it.'

We met Orval at one of our seminars where he had come to see whether the Witches could help him with his problem. We asked him about the days on which he had succeeded in picking even a few winners; for we knew that there must have been at least some occasions when he had good luck. Although at first he denied it (as indeed you may too), still after a lot of thought he was able to come up with some dates that had been lucky for him. (Even if your life has been as negative as Orval's, still you to can find a few good days to remember if you really try hard enough.) From those dates we were able to extract a lucky number for Orval. We were able to show him how to use that personalized lucky number to pick the winners he needed. At the same time we told him to go through a Sagittarian rebirth procedure and to choose a new name for himself so that he could cast off the image of a loser and get the image of a winner.

Orval chose his father's name to be reborn with, and now he is known as "Lucky Harry II."

Finding Your Own Lucky Number

Numerology is a very complex and exact science, one which we have studied for many years. There are both elaborate and simple methods of using its techniques; most of them rely on the reduction of large numbers to small numbers by addition of the digits. As an example, take a number like 873923. To find your lucky number from this demonstration number, you add its digits together as shown in Figure XI-2. Then add together the digits of the answer, the 3 and the 2, to arrive at your lucky number of 5.

There are two ways in which you can now find your own personal lucky number for any day of the month or year.

Procedure 1—Remember the time when you last had good luck. Write down the time to the nearest hour, and the date. If the time is between two hours, use the next following hour (the later hour of the two). If the time was between midnight and 1 a.m., use the number 25 for it. The hour must be expressed in terms of the 24-hour clock; i.e., 3 p.m. is 12 + 3, or 15—what the military call fifteen-hundred hours.

Let us say that your good luck occurred at 2:35 p.m. on the 28th day of July 1973. This reduces to the number 7, as shown in Figure XI-3. This is your basic lucky number. When you wish to have good luck at a specific time in the future, write down the hour, the day, the month, the year when it would be most appropriate for that good luck to occur. Let us say you wish the good luck to occur on the 5th day of January 1981 at 7:05 p.m. This gives you a 9, as shown in Figure XI-4. Add this number to your lucky number and again reduce it to a single digit as shown in Figure XI-5. Thus the lucky number for the event that you wish to occur is 7. You should write 7's at every available opportunity as the event approaches. Think of 7; carry 7's with you; and you will achieve the good fortune you seek.

Procedure 2—If you cannot remember any dramatically lucky day in your life, you must start with your birthdate. Reduce your birthdate in the way we have shown you, and add to it 22, which is considered by numerologists to be the Number of the Master. 22 is *the* superlative number, the number of the

8	
+ 7	
+ 3	
+ 9	
+ 2	3
+ 3	+ 2
32	5

Figure XI-2
Reducing Numbers

Hour	15 (12 + 2:35 i.e. 3)	2
Day	28	0
Month	7	2
Year	1973	3
	2023	7

Figure XI-3
Calculating Your Lucky Number

Hour	20 (7:05 or 8:00 + 12 hours)	2
Day	5	0
Month	1 (January)	0
Year	1981	7
	2007	9

Figure XI-4
Calculating the Time You Need Your Luck

9 (Target Event)	1
+ 7 (Your Ongoing Lucky Number)	+6
16	7

Figure XI-5
Identifying Your Lucky Event

truly great man, the man who combines superhuman personality characteristics with brilliance, driving energy, and abundant good fortune.

Gaining the Victory in Thy Race of Life

In my country as in thine, the winner of the race is remembered and rewarded. But in my country it is also true that we rewarded those who ran and lost if they showed great courage. Often we rewarded those courageous ones more than the professional athletes who had no difficulty in succeeding; for we recognized that even though a few can be brilliantly successful, still if the nation is to be great, all must strive toward perfection. Thou needest not to 'win' the race of life in order to have all that thou couldst possibly desire. Thou must, though, prepare thyself and run thy race with courage and perseverance. When thou dost persevere thou wilt assuredly be blessed by abundant good fortune. When thou art about to enter the race, thou wouldst indeed be foolish if thou didst not use every means at thy disposal to assure thyself of a place in the forefront of the finishers. Do not hesitate to use all the techniques I have described and all that Allah in His wisdom hath provided. Nor shouldst thou limit thyself to only one technique; for when thou usest more than one in combination, the effects do multiply and thou art assured of success.

Some Very Recent Examples of Astromantic Success

Mail from our students and from other people involved in the occult world comes to us by the sackful. We think it will be interesting for you to see some of the things people have achieved by applying Astromantic techniques—without any real formal training in the art.

1. *Alvin Marries the Girl of His Dreams*

Alvin T was your typical acne-ridden teenager of the 1960's. In seeking a cure for his acne, he learned of the techniques of color healing and astrological healing. This combination of healing you learned in Chapter V. He got rid of his acne through these techniques and at the same time improved his basic health, vigor, and vitality. Following up on the knowledge he gained, he acted like the magpie Gemini and enormously enlarged his circle of friends. Within this circle of friends he found the lady of his dreams. In a time when such things were still not approved, the two of them lived together for more than a year before becoming soul-mated in a Witches' handfasting. They are still today two of the most dedicated and happy people we know of in the occult scene.

2. *Wynne Wins the Sweepstakes Using Her Lucky Number*

Wynne E was a youngster who always dreamed of being a movie star. She came from a poor sharecropping family in Arkansas, though; and even if he had had the money, her father would not have tried to help Wynne to her 'sinful' dream. Wynne's worst problem was that she had the most frightful buck teeth, and the best estimate that the local orthodontist would give her for correction of this disfigurement ran to several thousand dollars. Wynne was mathematically inclined, and through her interest in mathematics became interested in the science of numerology. In a method similar to the one which we described, she developed her lucky number. From this she was able to buy a winning sweepstakes ticket. With the money she got from the sweepstakes, she had the necessary dental work done. This allowed her to become a TV personality.

Breaking into the TV world was not all that easy for Wynne, of course, even after she had the orthodontal work done. She used her lucky number many times in her search for fame, and she told us that every time she did the calculations correctly, she gained her objective.

3. *Geoffrey Sells a Worthless Inheritance for $3,000,000*

Geoffrey L was a fisherman in a small east coast town. He owned a little boat and a mobile home, but beyond this—nothing. He always dreamed of taking his boat to the Caribbean, where he would meet some island ladies and settle down in a tropical paradise. The necessities of eating and keeping up payments barred him from fulfilling his dream.

Geoffrey also owned the deed to some 25 acres of scrub land on the far outskirts of the county seat. He never believed that this piece of land, which he had inherited from his grandfather, would be worth anything; several years he had great difficulty even in raising the money to pay the minimal taxes on it.

Suddenly rumors flooded the county about a new freeway to the coast and the possibility of a shopping mall. When Geoffrey saw the proposed routes for the freeway, he noticed that one of them ran very close to the scrub land he owned. Now Geoffrey was no mean occultist; and even though he had never used any of the techniques he had read so much about, he determined that this time he would make things come out his way. First he attempted to influence the selection of the freeway routes. When the state government finally announced the selection, he was overjoyed to see that the one which would most benefit him had been chosen. Then it came down to whether he could sell his land to the real estate developers for the shopping center. Even though he used his best techniques, still he seemed to be failing. Then suddenly he remembered he ought to be building luck into his procedures. When he added lucky Sagittarius techniques to the procedure he had used earlier, all flowed smoothly. The land which had previously been worthless was sold for something over $3,000,000. Needless to say, Geoffrey is now contentedly basking in the warm Bahamian sun.

Overwhelming Insurmountable Objects with Astromancy

This book has given you everything you need with which to gain your objectives. Even if your dream objective seems unattainable today, still provided you start down the path toward gaining it, you use the techniques we have given you, and you add to them a little necessary luck, you will eventually arrive either at your present goal or at a goal even more desirable. Let us review the steps you should take.

1. Review your life's plan as we told you (Chapter II). Change your nature, either for a short time (Chapter I) or for a long time (Chapter III) so that you can easily attain your objective.

2. Now add Sagittarius lucky energies to your work. These are easily added by using the symbol disk from Chapter I or, if you need more, by following the procedure we gave you in this chapter to develop a lucky piece or Mojo.

3. Develop and use your lucky number. Do not ever overlook the power of the numbers; for in the heart of the numbers lies the secret of the universe.

Chapter Twelve

ENERGIZE YOUR NEW TREE OF LIFE WITH ASTROMANCY

The Difficulties along the Way

Men come to me and cry out, "When can I rest?" Even I who have passed into the spirit world am forced still to labor, still to learn by teaching others. The little children in their freedom bring bondage on themselves by playing games which follow definite rules; yet from these games they begin to learn about the world of man. Thus it is also with thy spirit. If it were set no tasks, it would learn naught. It would be as a child that stayeth as a child, that never learneth to take even the first step but is always dependent on its mother for life and sustenance. Thy Father Allah is wiser than that. He setteth tasks for His children so they may learn and find their way fulfilled in the world of the spirit. If thou dost reject the tasks thy Father setteth thee, He will assuredly send thee back to earth in some future time so that thou mayest learn them. Hiding from the tasks, refusing to take them, becoming dependent on someone else, even on thy government or thy family or thy mate, doth not allow thee to fulfill thyself.

Thou canst not grow if thine eyes are forever cast downward. Look unto the Wheel of the Heavens above thy head; and by understanding this great mystery thou canst grow. Be not afeared of thy failures; for even when thou dost not succeed, thou wilt learn by thine error and proceed to accomplish and grow more confidently upward.

Karen Fails to Qualify

Student File 1G-6WQ

Karen L is a student who lives on the Outer Banks of North Carolina. She has four elder brothers; all her life she and her brothers roamed like gypsies along the seashore. They all loved the sea. Karen studied our religion because she found in it more understanding of the ways of nature than in any other religion she had come across. She was not interested in the magical side of Witchcraft; only in what it had to teach about the balance of nature, about compassion to other living creatures, and about living in a non-damaging way on this planet.

As soon as they were able, two of her brothers joined the Coast Guard; and Karen's one ambition in life was also to join that organization. As a woman she knew that she would be facing stiff competition. She went to various sea schools; she trained herself in all the skills her fond brothers told her she would need. She becae perhaps obsessed with the idea of becoming a Coast Guard cadet. Finally she was interviewed, but was told she was not tall enough—a qualification she had not even thought about. She was shattered. Fortunately we were in Ocracoke shortly after this happened to her, and looked her up because we had not heard from her in a long while though she had previously been a very faithful correspondent. She told us of her shattered dreams and hopes one night as we all sat in the dunes looking at the moonlight across Silver Lake. As we talked, we hinted at other lines of work she might take, but she would not even discuss or consider anything other than the Coast Guard.

What Karen really wanted was some Witchcraft magic to make her taller. We told her as gently as we could that the magic didn't work on the body, it worked only on the spirit; and it is up to the spirit of the body to make what changes it can, whether it be healing, luck, wealth, or whatever. We told her very frankly that we did not think her spirit would make her taller but that she could learn from her experience and grow spiritually from understanding it.

Today Karen is a much-respected park ranger. She finds far more fulfillment in this job, dealing with sick animals and training youngsters, than we think she would have in the Coast Guard with its occasional negative police duty kind of work.

Finding Your Place

You may think the fates were unkind to Karen. Hereditarily she was born with genes which meant she would be of short stature; this made her physically handicapped when it came to fulfilling her desires. You are fated with certain physical characteristics. Included in these physical characteristics is your mind. Similarly you are fitted at birth with a certain type of spirit. As your body and your mind grow, so should your spirit; however, spiritual growth is largely neglected in the western world. The emphasis on the perfect body, tall, statuesque, sunburned, and a shallow mind to go with it, seems to be the highest aspiration of the way the majority of children are trained today. Spiritual training to test and develop this most important part of yourself is totally lacking.

Children are taught that they must win in every encounter. They are not taught how to have the necessary spiritual strength to accept defeat—let alone develop their spirit on their own outside of a competitive situation. Nowadays too, we are progressively arranging for the minds of our children to be shallower and duller. In our school systems, brilliance is at best ignored, and the brilliant child is often placed in classes with the mentally retarded so that all shall come out with an equally poor mind and none shall rise above the general low and mediocre level.

The mind is an amazing thing. When it is faced with more difficult problems to overcome, it can often achieve undreamed-of brilliance. Yet place it in an area where it is not exercised, and it becomes dull and empty. The mind and its intelligence are what sets us apart from lower animals. If you wish to climb a tree, you can go and get a ladder to help you. If your body is not tall enough to reach the fruit, by using your intelligence you can still get it. The first decision you must make in your steps to a new and better life is: What are the limits of your body? If you are too short, don't try to get into jobs that require tall people.

The Sweet Fruit of the Date-Palm Can Be Thine

Why art thou still groveling at the feet of another? Stand up. Look around thee. There are many who are worse off than thyself. What is it that holdeth thee back? Look upward to the stars, and see therein the power and the glory that thy Father Allah placed there. Art thou afeared to stand up and show thy face? Must thou forever hide in a burqa?[1] *Art thou afeared that some lesser mortal will laugh at thee if thou dost attempt and fail a task? The laughter will not hurt thee except in thine own imagination; and I can assure thee that this laughter helpeth thy spirit grow. If thou canst face down thy detractors, thou art truly a hero of the spirit and in this heroism thou art more courageous than he who merely faceth a physical danger as when the caravan is attacked by lions. Mayhap*

[1]Burqa: a tent-like overgarment.

thou fearest death; but death, as the great Sufis have said, is only thy chance to progress. I myself am 'dead;' yet still I labor in other planes. Still I must overcome mine own shortcomings—shortcomings now only of the spirit, though still as real as if I had a body to drag along with me. When I did live in the desert, I most feared pain. Pain is a sharp and terrible thing; but that too thou canst overcome. A strong spirit will overcome pain far more quickly and with more assurance than any drug; and unless thou art contemplating a career as a warrior, thou wilt not be expected to endure more pain than thou canst endure.

The Twenty-Two Faces of Eve

You may have read the book called "Three Faces of Eve;" it is a study of a woman who has multiple personalities. Mrs. Sizemore (for that is "Eve's" name) is now touring the country lecturing to various clinics on the results of the experiments that were conducted on "Eve." These multiple personalities give us an ideal opportunity to study the effect of spiritual changes on a single body; for Mrs. Sizemore existed in her alternate personalities for many years and spent long hours in each personality; in each identity she was subjected to batteries of psychological and mechanical tests. The results of those tests astounded the doctors who were running them. Take mental ability as an example: Mrs. Sizemore's IQ ranged from 80 to near 200; that is, from the level of slight mental retardation to well past genius, as she changed her spiritual characteristics. Three of the personalities were artists, all of whom painted in different styles. One of them was considered by art critics to be brilliant. From the personal point of view, in one or two personalities Mrs. Sizemore was, to put it quite frankly, a lewd nymphomaniac who would do everything she could to get a man into bed with her. In other personalities she was chaste and untouchable, and in fact seemed to dislike men. One of the things which amused the doctors (but was very annoying to Mrs. Sizemore) was that some of the personalities had extremely poor mechanical skills, to such an extent that some could not cook while others could; some could drive and others could not. This latter situation got Mrs. Sizemore into difficulties because she might for instance drive to town—but then be completely incapable of driving home again when a personality took over that was unable even to start the car.

As Mrs. Sizemore's personalities changed, so did her posture and her facial expression; however, her basic body parameters did not change. The spiritual changes gave her attributes that were within the capabilities of her body. Among the personalities were several which she could have used to become a successful artist, a businesswoman, or even a courtesan—if they had stayed with her.

Living to Your Potential

You may think that your body and mind hold you back from success. Mrs. Sizemore's case clearly shows that the only thing which holds you back is your spirit. This book has shown you how to change your spirit or modify it for short periods of time so that you can succeed in any endeavor. You too can increase your IQ or become an artist or, if you so desire, dramatically change your patterns of sexual behavior.

Throughout your upbringing in this western democracy, you have been trained to win; but even to get all you need, you do not have to win! A second, third, fourth, or even a fiftieth place is more than adequate. Look at any career that you wish to undertake. You do not have to be the absolute 'best' in the field in order to live comfortably and to gather around you many admirers. You can be successful in any endeavor that you undertake, provided only that you pick the spiritual attributes which are correct for that endeavor. Astromancy allows you easily to pick the attributes you need.

As you start along this path toward your goals, you need to analyze your own body and define for yourself just what it is you really want to do. The goal and your capabilities should be reconcilable to each other. If you have a genuine physical handicap that will prevent you attaining your goal, then change your goal to one that is attainable.

We often criticize the American educational system. This criticism is not to say that the system is not good; it is merely our attempt to push the system toward being even better: an antidote to complacency. Your education is undoubtedly better than that received by 90 percent of the rest of the world. If you believe your education is holding you back here, go somewhere else where you will be a shining light. If you are only a minor success in the highly competitive world of the big city, move to a smaller town. Many people find, as the old saying goes, that it is better to be a big frog in a small pond than a small frog in a big pond.

The spirit controls the mind, and the mind controls the body. Of the readers of this book, 99 percent have the mentality and the body to succeed; it is in the spiritual area they are lacking. It is in precisely this area that Astromancy comes to your aid. Pick what you want to do. Change the spirit as you have been taught, and you can hardly help succeeding.

The Caravan Gathereth Its Strength before Departure

The desert is indeed a frightful place. The good God placed it on earth as a test of man's enduring spirit. In every life there are material, emotional, and spiritual deserts. It is thy task on this earth to carry thyself and thy companions across these deserts. Thou canst learn from seeing the caravan as it prepareth to set out across the Arabian desert how thou shouldst approach these times of tribulation. Before the caravan departeth, every item that may be needed on the journey receiveth careful preparation and testing.

As the caravan prepareth and testeth itself, so must thou look for the hidden weaknesses that may make thee falter and lose thy way in the midst of the desert's hazardous sands. Hast thou reserves of food that will sustain thee through a period when thou wilt perhaps lack work? Hast thou the emo-

tional reserves that will carry thee surely across the time when thou dost lose a dear one? And above all, hast thou the spiritual strengths that will allow thee to adjust thy life to meet the times when fortune smileth not on thee? Where art thou today? Sittest thou on the brink of great experiences, letting them pass thee by?

Have no fear. Step out and honestly review thy life and what thou art best fitted for. If thou hast minor problems, take time to overcome them before thou startest on the journey; for once thou hast embarked, thou shouldst not turn back. Assuredly as thou crossest the deserts of thy life, thou shouldst revitalize thyself by supping at the oases along the way; but do not be distracted by the pleasures of the oasis until thou hast reached thy goal. For at thy goal all the pleasures of the world will be thine.

Again I ask thee: What is it that holdeth thee back from attaining bountiful reward for thine honest labor? Most men never move from their native village. They fear the desert. Fearest thou something along the way? And is not this why thou stayest in thine own small place?

Benjie the Ten-Year-Old Runs His Own Business

When Gavin was in the aerospace business, he once paid a visit to Pakistan to assess local industries and their capabilities to produce on-site some rather complex radar equipment. One of the firms that he was strongly urged to employ for making certain complex metal works was located in Lahore. (It was on this visit to Lahore that the tapes were made which are the underlying basis for this book.) That company employed a very youthful crew, and its principal trade was in brass and aluminum ware for local and tourist markets. The employees of the firm could in fact beat out by hand circular brass urns from single sheets of brass that were stunningly precise. All this was accomplished by beating the metal with a hammer on a leather-covered anvil. But Gavin could never quite get to the president of this metal-fabricating company.

Now Gavin was familiar with the stories in the United States of youngsters running their own little paper business, writing newsletters, selling lemonade, and the like; but he was astounded when he finally met the company president in Lahore to find out that he was only ten years old.

Benjie was undoubtedly a genius at organizing his young friends into a business. He told Gavin how it had all happened. He had come to the States with his father, who was learning to be an air-traffic controller. While in the States he had seen the mass-production techniques used to produce electronic equipment, much of which in those days was hand-assembled. With a brilliance far beyond his years, Benjie recognized that since Pakistan's labor rates were infinitesimal compared with those of the United States, people in Pakistan should be able to assemble equipment for a fraction of the cost for which it was done in the States.

He talked endlessly to his father about this; but the father was obstinate in his refusal to lend Benjie money or to help him get started. Thus Benjie turned to the better-known metal trade, where he saw that many tourist items were being made by craftsmen in the bazaar one at a time. He gathered a group of his friends around him, and with his small savings he bought some brass to found his own company. Despite many setbacks, he persisted; and in less than a year he had more than twenty youngsters in his own age group working for him, as well as his own father, who kept the books and made sure the boys stayed within the law.

Benjie's drive came, we believe, from the rebirth experience that he underwent when he visited America. For when he first arrived he became very ill, his stomach perhaps rejecting the unfamiliar foods. He was confined to hospital with a high fever. This fever left him and he grew well again on 5 April 1970, which made him an Aries. With the Aries' high drive he succeeded in his ambition. With his changed spirit, the body of even a nine-year-old was good enough to start the work which made Benjie the president of his own firm at the age of ten.

Cast Off Your Shell of Fear

Surely you are better equipped than Benjie to succeed in any endeavor you choose. Benjie may have been in some ways a child prodigy, but at nine years old he certainly did not have a developed mentality or body. It may be that the lack of development prevented him from seeing all those reasons why he 'could not do' something; and certainly at his young age he had far fewer of the fears which hold back so many adults from ultimate achievement.

Let us look at a list of typical fears (Table XII-1) that people use as reasons for not venturing forth. These are the well-known fears that have been documented and catalogued time and again by experimental psychologists. Notice how they are categorized into body fears and spiritual fears. As you glance down the list, you will see that the spiritual fears are the ones which are really most inhibiting. Probably the last one, fear of disappointment, is the most important. Opposite this list of fears we have placed the astrological sign which you can use to best advantage in overcoming any particular fear.

Take a moment now to go down the list and number your fears. Pick the one which you fear most and place a (1) against it. Now pick the one which you fear least, and place a (15) against that one. Now choose the second most feared experience and place a (2) against it. Now go out—today—and follow the advice in Chapter I to get yourself an image that will overcome your Number One fear. Next week, overcome your Number Two fear. When you have successfully overcome those two fears, you will be well on the way to proceeding into a more adventurous and fulfilling life.

Most Prevalent Fears	Nature Used to Overcome Fear	
Change	Aries	♈
Being sexually used	Scorpio	♏
Not having a partner	Gemini	♊
Being abandoned	Cancer	♋
Failing	Leo	♌
Being considered aggressive	Pisces	♓
Getting old	Aquarius	♒
Having uncontrollable anger	Virgo	♍
Getting fat	Libra	♎
Being too short	Libra	♎
Not fulfilling yourself	Capricorn	♑
Being sexually or otherwise incompetent	Scorpio	♏
Being laughed at	Sagittarus	♐
Losing money	Taurus	♉
Being disappointed	Pisces	♓

Table XII-1
Overcoming Fear

Progressing from Oasis to Oasis

The desert, the mountains, the sea, the icefields of the north: All are terrains which thou must be able to conquer if thou art to explore the world. Likewise if thou art to explore thy full potential, there are many different areas which thou must fit thyself to conquer. Just as the explorer learneth to take a ship across the great ocean and a camel across the desert, thou must learn to change thy spirit so that thou canst safely traverse all of life's hazards. It benefiteth thee nothing to take the outward garb of a desert dweller to the glaciers of the north. Thou wouldst indeed be foolish to do such a thing. Understand what it is thou needest to achieve any oasis, and then fit thy spirit for its laborsome journey. If thou fittest thy spirit properly, it will bring along with it the house thou livest in, which thou callest thy body. Understand the needs of thy spirit, and allow thy spirit to guide thy life. Get away from the buildings of men which are built only to satisfy their vanity. Get out where thou canst see the Wheel of the Heavens as it revolveth above thy head. Lift thine eyes to the spiritual truths of which I have told thee, and step briskly over the small obstacles which mundane men would place in thy path.

Michael's New Life Provides Wealth, Love, and Serenity

Student File 4Y-9DE

Michael Y came to us with a very sad story to tell. He was a brilliant scholar; not only that, but he was also a great athlete. In his young days he had become well known as a quarterback on the college football circuit, and he was picked up by a professional team as soon as he left college. However, after two years in the professionals, no one wanted him. Yes, he was a great player; but he just didn't have that competitive fire that is needed to smash down the opposition.

Although Michael was disappointed in his failure to make it big in the professional leagues, still he recognized his shortcomings and he moved into a partnership spot with a computer-programming firm. Gradually this partnership went sour and the business began to fail. At this point in his life Michael married a charming Libra lady who seemed to reinforce Michael's non-competitive nature; however, his marriage placed certain monetary strains on Michael's life. He wrote to us basically looking for a spell to gain him wealth, and indeed he did such a spell and gained enough money to overcome his immediate problems. In this way he became interested in the other precepts of our religion. The one which he could not really understand was that we were not in favor of turning the other cheek and letting the opposition run over us.

Michael had learned, and he conceived of it as a spiritual good, that he should never compete and that he should always take what life handed to him, accept it, and never question why he was continually a loser. It took us many months of discussion by letter and finally a personal interview with Michael in Minneapolis to convince him that his attitude was really very negative and that if he was to learn all of life's lessons he must learn the competitive aspects as well as the passive ones. Protesting, Michael cited Mohandas Gandhi as a great hero who overcame great obstacles with a pacifist approach; but we pointed out to Michael that by existing for many days without eating, for instance, Gandhi learned many other of life's spiritual lessons even though he was a pacifist. Being a pacifist did not mean that you should stop your spiritual development, we told him; and in the United States one good path to spiritual development is through competition. Competing hard and accepting losses makes the spirit grow; and not only does it make your spirit grow, but when you win it encourages growth in the spirits of those against whom you have competed.

Michael heeded our advice, and took on the spiritual image of a Leo in his business affairs. By doing this the business rapidly improved. A company that had been easy to outmaneuver suddenly seemed to be in the forefront of competitive bidding in the aerospace industry. Michael's spirit had grown beyond passivity into strength.

Dump the Parasites and Live

The key point that we learned from Michael's story is this: In order to succeed, you may perhaps have to teach other people that they cannot forever load you down. When people rely totally on a government or on another person to support them, they are not growing. If you have such parasites sucking off you, for their sake you should get rid of them; for they will not ever make spiritual progress while they rely on your beneficence.

Plan your life. Overcome your fears. Prepare yourself for the journey, as Ibn Saud taught, across the desert from oasis to oasis. In such a journey, can you afford to carry parasites with you? The most damaging of these parasites is undoubtedly the fear of not succeeding and the fear that you may 'sin' against some cosmic law. In recent years we have seen how things which in the past were 'deadly sins,' such as eating meat on Friday, have now—by the word not of God but of man—become blameless. Can you honestly say that these fears and 'sins' are not just excuses? Could it be that you really want to stay where you are? Or do you want to venture out and succeed? If you want to remain in the slough of despond, do not try to climb out. If you never start the journey, if you do not take the first step, you will never reach even the closest objectives. If you want success, the techniques in this book will give it to you; so try them honestly and give them time to work. Inshallah!